# SCRIPTURE JOURNAL

## STUDY EDITION

### ENGLISH STANDARD VERSION

# ROMANS

**CROSSWAY**

WHEATON, ILLINOIS — ESV.ORG

RRDS    34    33    32    31    30    29    28    27    26    25    24    23

14    13    12    11    10    9    8    7    6    5    4    3    2    1

# HOW TO USE THIS JOURNAL

How can you dig deeper into God's Word? Understand it better? Apply it well? Keep these fourteen foundational Bible study principles in mind when you read.

### 1. Start with Prayer

Starting with prayer might seem obvious, but it is incredibly important. On one difficult Bible passage J. C. Ryle wrote, "All portions of Scripture like this ought to be approached with deep humility and earnest prayer for the teaching of the Spirit." That is good advice for approaching tricky texts. But it is also good advice anytime you approach God's holy Word. Such a prayer is traditionally called a prayer of illumination, which typically focuses on asking the Holy Spirit to help you understand and rightly apply the Spirit-inspired Scriptures. For example, you could use or adapt this prayer: "Spirit of God, I know that your inspired Word is a lamp to my feet and a light to my path. Renew my mind to understand these words, soften my heart to love you, and strengthen my will to follow in your ways."

*Pray before you read!*

### 2. Stay with Prayer

Let God's Word lead you to pray. For example, after you read Jesus' prayer in Matthew 11:25 ("I thank you, Father, Lord of heaven and earth, that you have hidden these things from the wise and understanding and revealed them to little children"), thank him that he has revealed his "gracious will" (v. 26) to you. Praise him that you, through faith, are a child of God! You might also pray a Bible prayer directly, like the Lord's Prayer. Or write your own prayer based on whatever passage you have just read. For example, after reading Jesus' woes to the scribes and Pharisees in Matthew 23, pray that God would protect you from false teachers, keep you humble, and remind of you what matters most.

*Let Scripture guide your prayers.*

### 3. Look Godward

Often when we come to the Bible, our goal is application: "How should we live in light of what we have learned?" This is good, but, before you get there, turn your attention upward—Godward! Ask and answer questions like the following: What does this passage show me about God and his character? What does God do or say, love or hate, in this passage? What motivates God to do what he does?

*When you read God's Word, look Godward.*

### 4. Keep Christ as the Center

How would you define the gospel? Take a look at Jesus' summary to his first followers:

> Then he said to them, "These are my words that I spoke to you while I was still with you, that everything written about me in the Law of Moses and the Prophets and the Psalms must be fulfilled." Then he opened their minds to understand the Scriptures, and said to them, "Thus it is written, that the Christ should suffer and on the third day rise from the dead, and that repentance for the forgiveness of sins should be proclaimed in his name to all nations, beginning from Jerusalem. You are witnesses of these things." (Luke 24:44–48)

To Jesus, the gospel is grounded in the Old Testament; witnessed in history; centered on his sufferings, death, and resurrection; and proclaimed to the nations so to require a response: to repent of sin and receive, through faith, the forgiveness of sins.

*According to Jesus, the gospel about Jesus is the unifying interpretive center of the Scriptures. So, as you read, always ask this question: How does the section declare, reflect on, or apply the gospel?*

### 5. Look for Biblical-Theological Themes

The Bible is not a disjointed group of sayings and stories that are randomly placed together, but it is a grand story of God's work in the history of salvation. So when you read the New Testament, you must be aware that the story it presents (the Messiah has come!) is building upon the story of the Old Testament (the Messiah will come). Major themes include the kingdom, exodus and exile, priest and temple, and the covenant. These themes, and others like them, develop progressively. They follow a historical trajectory (e.g., God's promise to bless the nations is fulfilled as the church makes disciples of all nations) but also include typological connections (e.g., Jesus

is the Passover Lamb, whose shed blood saves us from God's wrath) and ana-
logical connections (e.g., Jesus is greater than the temple, because he is the
great high priest, who sacrifices himself for sinners, and is the permanent
presence of God on earth and in God's people).

*Your task in reading (a tricky task at times!) is to consider how these biblical-theological
themes might be present in the passage you are reading and, as a result, how they might
connect to the gospel of Jesus Christ.*

### 6. Hear the Melodic Line

In music a melodic line is the tune within the tune—that is, a succession
of notes that creates a distinctive sound. Those notes are repeated regularly
and bring unity to the song. Each book of the Bible has its own unique
melodic line, and our task as readers is to find these author-placed notes,
understand them, and discover why they are played together. Think of the
key notes as key words (see the Glossary in the back if you need help!) and
the melodic line as the key themes. For example, a possible melodic line for
the Gospel of Mark could be *arise and follow the Son.* The word *Son* is a key
word, one that Mark begins with ("The beginning of the gospel of Jesus
Christ, the Son of God," Mark 1:1) and that he continues to come back to
at strategic points. As we read through this Gospel, we learn that Jesus is
the Son of God, the Son of David, and the Son of Man. The theme of Jesus'
identity matters to Mark. So too does the theme of discipleship—thus the
first part of the suggested melodic line: "Arise and follow." Throughout
the pages of this Gospel Jesus calls people to follow him, and he details
what that means (e.g., to deny self, to love others). Practically, knowing the
melodic line helps us understand each passage better because we understand how it relates to the overall theme of a book.

*So, as you read, keep an ear to the ground. Hear the melodic line.*

### 7. Trace the Argument

Not every book in the New Testament presents a linear and logical argument, as many of Paul's letters do. But making logical connections between
sections of a book, and within paragraphs and sentences, can help you
understand the author's message. There are many ways to trace an argument
to find the flow of thought. A common suggestion is, first, to isolate the idea
or assertion and, second, to notice the conjunctions and prepositions and try
to make sense of their relationship with the idea. For example, in Ephesians
5:18–21, after Paul offers a command ("Do not get drunk with wine") and
the reason to heed that command ("For that is debauchery"), he introduces

the main clause: "But be filled with the Spirit." In the following verse he explains some specific ways to be Spirit-filled and/or to express that the Spirit is at work. Paul introduces four subordinate or supporting clauses:

a. "addressing one another in psalms and hymns and spiritual songs"
b. "singing and making melody to the Lord with your heart"
c. "giving thanks always and for everything to God the Father"
d. "submitting to one another out of reverence for Christ."

*Of course, not every sentence or section of Scripture is written in such a logical way, but as we read we should seek to find how an author has crafted his message and should hope to identify and understand how each paragraph relates to the preceding and following ones.*

### 8. Read through the Lens of Love

In his classic work *De Doctrina Christiana* (*On Christian Doctrine*) Augustine said that the goal of biblical interpretation is determined by the church's "rule of faith"; that is, our understanding of Scripture must always be guided by our love for God and neighbor. Put differently, if we think a text is saying something that would keep us from love, then we have the wrong interpretation. Of course, Augustine's direction is based on Jesus' answer to the question "Which is the great commandment in the Law?" (Matt. 22:36), namely,

> You shall love the Lord your God with all your heart and with all your soul and with all your mind. This is the great and first commandment. And a second is like it: You shall love your neighbor as yourself. On these two commandments depend all the Law and the Prophets. (22:37–40)

The whole of the Old Testament ("All the Law and the Prophets")—and, we can add, all the New Testament too (see Paul on love's fulfilling the law in Rom. 13:8–10)—should be read through the lens of love. Of course, the laws of God (not stealing, not committing adultery, and so on) are laws of love—the way we love God and others is through keeping all his laws.

*So, let the Lord's lawful love lead!*

### 9. Let Scripture Interpret Scripture

Because we believe that "all Scripture is breathed out by God" (2 Tim. 3:16), we expect that the Bible's recording of historical people and events is accurate, its narrative cohesive, and its theology coherent. One of the great truths rediscovered in the Protestant Reformation was *Scriptura sacra sui ipsius interpres,* which is Latin for "Sacred Scripture is its own interpreter." Scripture interprets Scripture! The principle is that we use explicit or clear sections of Scripture to help us understand a more implicit or less clear section.

*As you read the Bible, let the Bible itself help you understand its proper meaning and application.*

### 10. Be Changed by Your Bible Reading

Reading the Bible should change us. Before Paul writes "All Scripture is breathed out by God" in 2 Timothy 3:16, he teaches us that "the sacred writings" can "make [us] wise for salvation through faith in Christ Jesus" (3:15). Put differently, the Bible is designed to give its readers saving faith. That is one of its goals. The other is to train us "in righteousness" and to equip us "for every good work" (3:16, 17). Bible reading should strengthen our faith and equip and encourage us to live out that faith in the church and the world.

*Therefore, we should "be doers of the word, and not hearers [or readers!] only" (James 1:22).*

### 11. Think of the Original Readers

It is easy, but wrong, to read the Bible and think that everything an author says to his original audience is meant for you today. Sometimes a text is directly applicable. We should love our neighbors today just as much as Jesus' first followers did then. But other times the author, or a character in the author's narrative, is addressing only his first hearers. For example, when our Lord predicts the destruction of the temple in his Olivet Discourse and then commands "those who are in Judea to flee to the mountains" (Matt. 24:16), he means that the Jewish Christians who live in or near Jerusalem in AD 70 should run for their lives and hide in the hills when the Romans come to town. And the next command ("Let the one who is on the [flat] housetop [common in that time and place] not go down to take what is in his house"; v. 17) has nothing to do with you, your house, and some escape plan!

*If we seek to interpret the Bible rightly, our interpretation must be based on the author's (or speaker's) original intention to his original readers. The text cannot mean something to us that it did not first mean to them.*

### 12. Grasp the Genres

A genre is simply a type of literature. Some of the prevalent genres in the Bible include narrative, poetry, epistle, proverb, and visionary writing.

Each genre comes with its own rules of interpretation, which can be over-whelming! But take heart—the more you read the Bible with an eye open for the different genres, the more you will start to see that different books should be read differently. For example, you will come to understand that visionary writing uses images and metaphors as symbols—and thus that the depiction of Jesus in Revelation 1 (with "a sharp two-edged sword" coming from "his mouth," Rev. 1:16) symbolizes something about Jesus as judge. In contrast, Jesus' washing his disciples' feet in John 13 is a literal historical record of an event that happened.

*So when you read a passage, consider what genre it is in order to discern what it is emphasizing and how you should apply it to your life.*

### 13. Study the Context

As you read, seek to understand who wrote a book, when it was written, to whom it was written, and why it was written. That is the historical context, and the book introductions will cover such significant details. Also, use the study notes when you need light shed on people, places, and events far removed from our day. For example, when the Gospels talk about "lawyers," they are referencing "experts in the Law of Moses" (the first five books of the Bible). The literary context is important as well. Literary context simply refers to what surrounds a text (what is said or happens in the verses before and after) and where the text is found in the whole of the book. For exam-ple, Jesus told the parable of the rich man and Lazarus (Luke 16:19–31), in part, as a rebuke and warning to the Pharisees, who Luke informs us "were lovers of money" and who "ridiculed" Jesus (v. 14) after he taught the parable of the dishonest manager (vv. 1–13), which concludes: "No servant can serve two masters, for either he will hate the one and love the other, or he will be devoted to the one and despise the other. You cannot serve God and money."

*In sum, if you know the historical and literary context of the passage, you will have a better understanding of its meaning.*

### 14. Read in Community

The Word of God is for the people of God and is meant to be read, stud-ied, and lived out in community. So, like Israel of old, God's people should gather around God's Word to be instructed by God's appointed leaders. (After "all the people gathered" to hear from "the Book of the Law of Moses that the LORD had commanded Israel" [Neh. 8:1], the Bible was read "clearly" and explained as the scribes "gave the sense, so that the people understood the reading," [8:8].) And, like the early church, we too should devote ourselves to "the apostles' teaching" (what became the New Testament) as we fellowship with each other (see Acts 2:42). So bring your Bible to church and listen and learn from good teachers and preachers. Also bring it to Bible study, share your thoughts, and let others help you discover truths you might have missed.

*As you read together, you will grow together!*

# PREFACE

## *The Bible*

"This Book [is] the most valuable thing that this world affords. Here is Wisdom; this is the royal Law; these are the lively Oracles of God." With these words the Moderator of the Church of Scotland hands a Bible to the new monarch in Britain's coronation service. These words echo the King James Bible translators, who wrote in 1611, "God's sacred Word . . . is that inestimable treasure that excelleth all the riches of the earth." This assessment of the Bible is the motivating force behind the publication of the English Standard Version.

## *Translation Legacy*

The English Standard Version (ESV) stands in the classic mainstream of English Bible translations over the past half-millennium. The fountainhead of that stream was William Tyndale's New Testament of 1526; marking its course were the King James Version of 1611 (KJV), the English Revised Version of 1885 (RV), the American Standard Version of 1901 (ASV), and the Revised Standard Version of 1952 and 1971 (RSV). In that stream, faithfulness to the text and vigorous pursuit of precision were combined with simplicity, beauty, and dignity of expression. Our goal has been to carry forward this legacy for this generation and generations to come.

To this end each word and phrase in the ESV has been carefully weighed against the original Hebrew, Aramaic, and Greek, to ensure the fullest accuracy and clarity and to avoid under-translating or overlooking any nuance of the original text. The words and phrases themselves grow out of the Tyndale–King James legacy, and most recently out of the RSV, with the 1971 RSV text providing the starting point for our work. Archaic language has been brought into line with current usage and significant corrections have been made in the translation of key texts. But throughout, our goal has been to retain the depth of meaning and enduring quality of language that have made their indelible mark on the English-speaking world and have defined the life and doctrine of its church over the last five centuries.

*Translation Philosophy*

The ESV is an "essentially literal" translation that seeks as far as possible to reproduce the precise wording of the original text and the personal style of each Bible writer. As such, its emphasis is on "word-for-word" correspondence, at the same time taking full account of differences in grammar, syntax, and idiom between current literary English and the original languages. Thus it seeks to be transparent to the original text, letting the reader see as directly as possible the structure and exact force of the original.

In contrast to the ESV, some Bible versions have followed a "thought-for-thought" rather than "word-for-word" translation philosophy, emphasizing "dynamic equivalence" rather than the "essentially literal" meaning of the original. A "thought-for-thought" translation is of necessity more inclined to reflect the interpretive views of the translator and the influences of contemporary culture.

Every translation is at many points a trade-off between literal precision and readability, between "formal equivalence" in expression and "functional equivalence" in communication, and the ESV is no exception. Within this framework we have sought to be "as literal as possible" while maintaining clarity of expression and literary excellence. Therefore, to the extent that plain English permits and the meaning in each case allows, we have sought to use the same English word for important recurring words in the original; and, as far as grammar and syntax allow, we have rendered Old Testament passages cited in the New in ways that show their correspondence. Thus in each of these areas, as well as throughout the Bible as a whole, we have sought to capture all the echoes and overtones of meaning that are so abundantly present in the original texts.

As an essentially literal translation, taking into account grammar and syntax, the ESV thus seeks to carry over every possible nuance of meaning in the original words of Scripture into our own language. As such, the ESV is ideally suited for in-depth study of the Bible. Indeed, with its commitment to literary excellence, the ESV is equally well suited for public reading and preaching, for private reading and reflection, for both academic and devotional study, and for Scripture memorization.

*Translation Principles and Style*

The ESV also carries forward classic translation principles in its literary style. Accordingly it retains theological terminology—words such as grace, faith, justification, sanctification, redemption, regeneration, reconciliation, propitiation—because of their central importance for Christian doctrine and also because the underlying Greek words were already becoming key words and technical terms among Christians in New Testament times.

The ESV lets the stylistic variety of the biblical writers fully express itself—from the exalted prose that opens Genesis, to the flowing narratives of the historical books, to the rich metaphors and dramatic imagery of the poetic books, to the ringing rhetoric in the prophetic books, to the smooth elegance of Luke, to the profound simplicities of John, and the closely reasoned logic of Paul.

In punctuating, paragraphing, dividing long sentences, and rendering connectives, the ESV follows the path that seems to make the ongoing flow of thought clearest in English. The biblical languages regularly connect sentences by frequent repetition of words such as "and," "but," and "for," in a way that goes beyond the conventions of current literary English. Effective translation, however, requires that these links in the original be reproduced so that the flow of the argument will be transparent to the reader. We have therefore normally translated these connectives, though occasionally we have varied the rendering by using alternatives (such as "also," "however," "now," "so," "then," or "thus") when they better express the linkage in specific instances.

In the area of gender language, the goal of the ESV is to render literally what is in the original. For example, "anyone" replaces "any man" where there is no word corresponding to "man" in the original languages, and "people" rather than "men" is regularly used where the original languages refer to both men and women. But the words "man" and "men" are retained where a male meaning component is part of the original Greek or Hebrew. Likewise, the word "man" has been retained where the original text intends to convey a clear contrast between "God" on the one hand and "man" on the other hand, with "man" being used in the collective sense of the whole human race (see Luke 2:52). Similarly, the English word "brothers" (translating the Greek word *adelphoi*) is retained as an important familial form of address between fellow-Jews and fellow-Christians in the first century. A recurring note is included to indicate that the term "brothers" (*adelphoi*) was often used in Greek to refer to both men and women, and to indicate the specific instances in the text where this is the case. In addition, the English word "sons" (translating the Greek word *huioi*) is retained in specific instances because the underlying Greek term usually includes a male meaning component and it was used as a legal term in the adoption and inheritance laws of first-century Rome. As used by the apostle Paul, this term refers to the status of all Christians, both men and women, who, having been adopted into God's family, now enjoy all the privileges, obligations, and inheritance rights of God's children.

The inclusive use of the generic "he" has also regularly been retained, because this is consistent with similar usage in the original languages and because an essentially literal translation would be impossible without it.

In each case the objective has been transparency to the original text, allowing the reader to understand the original on its own terms rather than in the terms of our present-day Western culture.

### The Translation of Specialized Terms

The Greek word *Christos* has been translated consistently as "Christ." Although the term originally meant simply "anointed," among Jews in New Testament times it had specifically come to designate the Messiah, the great Savior that God had promised to raise up. In other New Testament contexts, however, especially among Gentiles, *Christos* ("Christ") was on its way to becoming a proper name. It is important, therefore, to keep the context in mind in understanding the various ways that *Christos* ("Christ") is used in the New Testament. At the same time, in accord with its "essentially literal" translation philosophy, the ESV has retained consistency and concordance in the translation of *Christos* ("Christ") throughout the New Testament.

Second, a particular difficulty is presented when words in biblical Greek refer to ancient practices and institutions that do not correspond directly to those in the modern world. Such is the case in the translation of *doulos*, a term which is often rendered "slave." This term, however, actually covers a range of relationships that requires a range of renderings—"slave," "bondservant," or "servant"—depending on the context. Further, the word "slave" currently carries associations with the often brutal and dehumanizing institution of slavery particularly in nineteenth-century America. For this reason, the ESV translation of the word *doulos* has been undertaken with particular attention to its meaning in each specific context. In New Testament times, a *doulos* is often best described as a "bondservant"—that is, someone in the Roman Empire officially bound under contract to serve his master for seven years (except for those in Caesar's household in Rome who were contracted for fourteen years). When the contract expired, the person was freed, given his wage that had been saved by the master, and officially declared a freedman. The ESV usage thus seeks to express the most fitting nuance of meaning in each context. Where absolute ownership by a master is envisaged (as in Romans 6), "slave" is used; where a more limited form of servitude is in view, "bondservant" is used (as in 1 Corinthians

7:21–24); where the context indicates a wide range of freedom (as in John 4:51), "servant" is preferred. Footnotes are generally provided to identify the Greek and the range of meaning that this term may carry in each case. The issues involved in translating the Greek word *doulos* apply also to the Greek word *sundoulos*, translated in the text as "fellow servant."

Third, it is sometimes suggested that Bible translations should capitalize pronouns referring to deity. It has seemed best not to capitalize deity pronouns in the ESV, however, for the following reasons: first, there is nothing in the original Greek manuscripts that corresponds to such capitalization; second, the practice of capitalizing deity pronouns in English Bible translations is a recent innovation, which began only in the mid-twentieth century; and, third, such capitalization is absent from the KJV Bible and the whole stream of Bible translations that the ESV carries forward.

A fourth specialized term, the word "behold," usually has been retained as the most common translation for the Greek word *idou*, which means something like "Pay careful attention to what follows! This is important!" Other than the word "behold," there is no single word in English that fits well in most contexts. Although "Look!" and "See!" and "Listen!" would be workable in some contexts, in many others these words lack sufficient weight and dignity. Given the principles of "essentially literal" translation, it is important not to leave *idou* completely untranslated and so to lose the intended emphasis in the original language. The older and more formal word "behold" has usually been retained, therefore, as the best available option for conveying the original weight of meaning.

### Textual Basis and Resources

The ESV New Testament is based on the Greek text in the 2014 editions of the *Greek New Testament* (5th corrected ed.), published by the United Bible Societies (UBS), and *Novum Testamentum Graece* (28th ed., 2012), edited by Nestle and Aland. In a few difficult cases in the New Testament, the ESV has followed a Greek text different from the text given preference in the UBS/ Nestle-Aland 28th edition. Throughout, the translation team has benefited greatly from the massive textual resources that have become readily available recently, from new insights into biblical laws and culture, and from current advances in Greek lexicography and grammatical understanding.

### Textual Footnotes

The footnotes that are included in most editions of the ESV are therefore an integral part of the ESV translation, informing the reader of textual variations and difficulties and showing how these have been resolved by the ESV translation team. In addition to this, the footnotes indicate significant alternative readings and occasionally provide an explanation for technical terms or for a difficult reading in the text.

### Publishing Team

The ESV publishing team has included more than a hundred people. The fourteen-member Translation Oversight Committee benefited from the work of more than fifty biblical experts serving as Translation Review Scholars and from the comments of the more than fifty members of the Advisory Council, all of which was carried out under the auspices of the Crossway Board of Directors. This hundred-plus-member team shares a common commitment to the truth of God's Word and to historic Christian orthodoxy and is international in scope, including leaders in many denominations.

### To God's Honor and Praise

We know that no Bible translation is perfect; but we also know that God uses imperfect and inadequate things to his honor and praise. So to our triune God and to his people we offer what we have done, with our prayers that it may prove useful, with gratitude for much help given, and with ongoing wonder that our God should ever have entrusted to us so momentous a task.

*Soli Deo Gloria!*—To God alone be the glory!

*The Translation Oversight Committee*

# ROMANS

### Author, Date, and Recipients

The apostle Paul wrote to the Christians in Rome. He probably did this while he was in Corinth on his third missionary journey, in AD 57 (Acts 20:2–3).

### Theme

In the cross of Christ, God judges sin and at the same time shows his saving mercy.

### Purpose

Paul wrote Romans to unite the Jewish and Gentile Christians in Rome in the gospel. He also wanted the church in Rome to become the base of operations from which he could proclaim the gospel in Spain (15:22–24). The ultimate goal of preaching the gospel is the glory of God (11:33–36). Paul longs for the Gentiles to become obedient Christians for the sake of Christ's name (1:5).

### The Gospel in Romans

In the sweep of the New Testament, Romans is the first epistle encountered. This is fitting, as it builds on the Old Testament, explains the saving work of Jesus reported in the Gospels, and unpacks many of the teachings that were foundational to the churches that arose in Acts. In these respects, Romans flows naturally from the biblical books preceding it.

Yet the epistle to the Romans holds a prominent place among all other biblical writings. First, it played a direct role in the conversion of such key figures in church history as Augustine, Martin Luther, and John Wesley. John Calvin wrote that Romans is the doorway to the treasure of all of Scripture.

Second, Romans is widely regarded as the most complete summary of the gospel message and Christian doctrine found in any single biblical book. It is certainly Paul's most extended and concentrated presentation of God's saving work in Christ.

Third, its overarching theme is the gospel message. That message is not merely useful information: it is no less than "the power of God for salvation to everyone who believes" (1:16). As God's sovereign word created the world (Genesis 1), so by God's message about his Son a creative and renewing "righteousness of God is revealed from faith for faith" (Rom. 1:17). To read Romans is to encounter a message able to elicit "the obedience of faith" (1:5; 16:26) in Jesus Christ from start to finish. This brings the righteousness Jesus established by his life and saving death to the sinner, to the church, and by extension to the whole world. If the mission of Jesus' followers is to carry his good news to all places, Romans is a key biblical book to take to heart.

Is there any way to summarize such a revolutionary, rich, and wide-ranging epistle? One approach to discovering what is most central in Romans is to note which significant nouns are used most frequently. Paul used these three words most often in Romans (word counts based on the original Greek text):

*God* (153 times). He is the subject around whom the entire epistle revolves. Romans lifts our gaze from the tyranny of our self-absorption to the grandeur of a God of kindness (2:4), faithfulness (3:3), truth (3:4), righteousness (3:5), and glory (3:7), to name just a few of his attributes. Yes, he is severe in judgment (11:22), yet through faith he is so dear that his people know him as "Abba" (8:15), their caring heavenly Father. They have "peace with God," they stand in his grace, and they "rejoice in hope of the glory of God" (5:1–2).

*Law* (74 times). Cultures may be diverse, but Scripture views humans of all cultures as having one thing profoundly in common: "all have sinned and fall short of the glory of God" (3:23). We have all broken God's "holy and righteous and good" commandment (7:12). Yet Romans trumpets that in sending "his own Son," God fulfilled what the law demanded but we humans could not furnish (8:3–4). Believers are liberated "in Christ Jesus from the law of sin and death" (8:2).

*Christ* (65 times; see also *Lord*, 43 times; *Jesus*, 36 times). The author of Romans is a slave or servant of Christ (1:1). His readers are "called to belong to Jesus Christ" (1:6). Next to "Amen," "Christ" is the last word of Romans (16:27). Through him God will "graciously give . . . all things" he has promised to those who are changed by the gospel message (8:32).

Romans is not only about weighty words piling up into lofty teachings. It is also about ethics—how to live. No chapter is without gospel-informed implications for daily living, with chapters 12–15 most suggestive in this regard. Similarly, Romans testifies repeatedly to divine love. We are creatures of devotion, created to know and to love the God who made us. Through the love unleashed by the gospel, poured into our hearts by the Holy Spirit (5:5), we join in the doxologies that dot the epistle (see 1:25; 9:5; 11:36), such as this one at the close: "to the only wise God be glory forevermore through Jesus Christ! Amen" (16:27).

### Romans and Christian Doctrine

A glimpse of the doctrinal treasures in Romans is afforded by a survey of seven aspects of its message:

1. *God and his gospel.* The beginning and end of Romans speak of good news from God: the gospel. This is a message "promised beforehand through his prophets in the holy Scriptures" (Rom. 1:2), a message that will "bring about the obedience of faith for the sake of his name among all the nations" (1:5; see also 16:25–26).

2. *Humanity and our need.* Immediately after Romans introduces the gospel (1:16–17), it speaks of the "wrath of God . . . revealed from heaven against all ungodliness and unrighteousness of men" (1:18), followed by a lengthy description of human sin and condemnation (1:18–3:20). The good news of Romans takes shape against the grim news of the human predicament.

3. *Christ and his work.* "The power of God for salvation" proclaimed in the gospel (1:16) centers on Jesus' death (3:24–26) and resurrection (4:25). He effects peace with God (5:1), as his sacrifice for sin opened up "access by faith into this grace in which we stand" (5:2). Our forefather in this faith was Abraham (ch. 4). Christ the second Adam undid the ruin the first Adam brought about (5:12–21). God "justifies the ungodly," so that faith in Christ, who died and rose, "is counted as righteousness" (4:5).

4. *The Spirit and his help.* The Holy Spirit played a role in the revelation of Jesus as Son of God by his resurrection after his execution (1:4). He was at work in the salvation of God's OT people (2:29). The Spirit pours out God's love into the hearts of those who are reconciled to God through faith in Christ (5:5). Twenty of the almost three dozen references to God's Spirit come in Romans 8. The Spirit infuses divine life into believing mortal humans (8:11), leads them (8:14), and intercedes where their own prayers falter and fail (8:26).

5. *God's word and its truth.* Romans 9–11 discusses issues raised by Christ's rejection by many Jews of his time. Did God's promises to them, his word,

somehow fail (9:6)? Did God turn his back on his covenant people of old in sending Jesus as the Messiah (11:1)? By extended and intense arguments, Romans assures readers of God's integrity, justice, and faithfulness to his character and promises. This theme recurs throughout Romans and is perhaps the main ground for repeated eruptions of doxology, where lofty praise of God is followed by "Amen" (1:25; 9:5; 11:36; 15:33; 16:27).

6. *God's people and their mission.* The gospel message is for all, both Jew and Greek (1:16; 2:9–10; 3:9; 10:12). Christ came for missionary purposes that involve his followers (15:8–13). Paul's "ambition to preach the gospel" (15:20) is shared by the church through the ages wherever Jesus' call to make disciples (Matt. 28:19–20) is heeded.

7. *God's love and its power.* God showed his love by Christ's death for the ungodly (Rom. 5:8). Nothing can separate believers from God's love in Christ (8:39).

### Literary Features

Romans contains all of the standard features of a biblical epistle, including the salutation, thanksgiving, body, *paraenesis* (list of moral exhortations), personal greetings, and benediction. What distinguishes the letter is its long and carefully constructed body, which presents a sustained theological argument. Romans is perhaps the most tightly organized of all the NT letters, which helps explain why it reads as much like a theological treatise as it does a letter. Understanding Romans thus demands careful attention to the details of its doctrine.

As a theological treatise, the book of Romans is a grand edifice. It is filled with lofty theological ideas and vocabulary. The rhetoric is often grand, taking such forms as elaborate sentence construction (syntax) and patterns of verbal repetition. What is often overlooked is that there is a continuous presence of a genre that tends toward the informal and that even lends a colloquial vigor that balances its grandeur. This genre, known as the diatribe, was used extensively by Roman teachers and orators (also known as preachers). The traits of the form included the following: dialogue with hypothetical questioners or opponents; as part of that, question-and-answer constructions, sometimes catechism-like in effect; use of questions or hypothetical objections as a transition to the next topic; rhetorical questions; adducing famous and representative figures from the past as examples; use of analogy as a rhetorical device; and aphoristic style.

The book is unified primarily by the coherence of its central argument, which outlines and explains the eternal plan of God for the salvation of sinners. The book's thesis statement (see 1:16–17) alerts the reader to the central place that the righteousness of God occupies in this plan—the righteousness that God both demands in obedience and offers as a free gift in Christ, received by faith.

### Key Themes

1. All people are sinners and need to be saved from their sin (1:18–3:20; 5:12–19).
2. The Mosaic law is good and holy, but only Christ can remove sin and overcome its power (2:12–29; 3:9–20; 5:20; 7:1–25; 9:30–10:8).
3. Through the righteousness of God, sin is judged and salvation is provided (3:21–26; 5:12–19; 6:1–10; 7:1–6; 8:1–4).
4. With the coming of Jesus Christ, a new age of redemptive history has begun (1:1–7; 3:21–26; 5:1–8:39).
5. The atoning death of Jesus Christ is central to God's plan of salvation (3:21–26; 4:23–25; 5:6–11, 15–19; 6:1–10; 7:4–6; 8:1–4).
6. Justification is by faith alone (1:16–4:25; 9:30–10:21).
7. Those who are in Christ Jesus have a sure hope of future glory (5:1–8:39).
8. By the power of the Holy Spirit, those who have died with Christ live a new life (2:25–29; 6:1–7:6; 8:1–39).
9. God is sovereign in salvation. He works all things according to his plan (9:1–11:36).
10. God fulfills his promises to both Jews and Gentiles (1:18–4:25; 9:1–11:36; 14:1–15:13).
11. Because of God's grace, Christians should be morally pure, should show love to their neighbors, should be good citizens, and should welcome their fellow believers into fullest fellowship (12:1–15:7).

### Outline

I. The Gospel as the Revelation of the Righteousness of God (1:1–17)
   A. Salutation: the gospel concerning God's Son (1:1–7)
   B. Thanksgiving: prayer for an apostolic visit (1:8–15)
   C. Theme: the gospel of the righteousness of God (1:16–17)

II. God's Righteousness in His Wrath against Sinners (1:18–3:20)
   A. The unrighteousness of the Gentiles (1:18–32)
   B. The unrighteousness of the Jews (2:1–3:8)
   C. The unrighteousness of all people (3:9–20)

III. The Saving Righteousness of God (3:21–4:25)
   A. God's righteousness in the death of Jesus (3:21–26)
   B. Righteousness by faith for Jews and Gentiles (3:27–31)
   C. Abraham as the father of Jews and Gentiles (4:1–25)

IV. Hope as a Result of Righteousness by Faith (5:1–8:39)
   A. Assurance of hope (5:1–11)
   B. Hope in Christ's triumph over Adam's sin (5:12–21)
   C. The triumph of grace over the power of sin (6:1–23)
   D. The triumph of grace over the power of the law (7:1–6)
   E. The law and sin (7:7–25)
   F. Life in the Spirit (8:1–17)
   G. Assurance of hope (8:18–39)

V. God's Righteousness to Israel and to the Gentiles (9:1–11:36)
   A. God's saving promises to Israel (9:1–29)
   B. Israel's rejection of God's saving promises (9:30–11:10)
   C. God's righteousness in his plan for Jews and Gentiles (11:11–32)
   D. Concluding doxology (11:33–36)

VI. God's Righteousness in Everyday Life (12:1–15:13)
   A. Paradigm for exhortations: total dedication to God (12:1–2)
   B. Marks of the Christian community (12:3–13:14)
   C. A call for mutual acceptance between the strong and the weak (14:1–15:13)

VII. The Extension of God's Righteousness through the Pauline Mission (15:14–16:23)
   A. The establishment of churches among the Gentiles (15:14–33)
   B. Appreciation and greetings to coworkers in the gospel (16:1–23)

VIII. Final Summary of the Gospel of the Righteousness of God (16:25–27)

### The Setting of Romans

# ROMANS

## Greeting

1 Paul, a servant[1] of Christ Jesus, called to be an apostle, set apart for the gospel of God, [2] which he promised beforehand through his prophets in the holy Scriptures, [3] concerning his Son, who was descended from David[2] according to the flesh [4] and was declared to be the Son of God in power according to the Spirit of holiness by his resurrection from the dead, Jesus Christ our Lord, [5] through whom we have received grace and apostleship to bring about the obedience of faith for the sake of his name among all the nations, [6] including you who are called to belong to Jesus Christ,

[1] For the contextual rendering of the Greek word *doulos*, see Preface  [2] Or *who came from the offspring of David*

**1:1–17 The Gospel as the Revelation of God's Righteousness.** This first section includes Paul's opening greeting (vv. 1–7), thanksgiving (vv. 8–15), and statement of the letter's overall theme (vv. 16–17).

**1:1–7** This is the longest introduction of any of Paul's letters. He has never been to Rome, so he summarizes the gospel for his Roman readers. Many of the things he mentions here are also in the final verses of his letter (16:25–27): (1) Paul's apostolic authority; (2) how the gospel fulfills OT Scriptures; (3) how the gospel centers on Jesus Christ; (4) the obedience of faith; (5) Paul's mission to the Gentiles; and (6) the glory of Jesus Christ and God the Father.

**1:1 Servant** indicates that Paul is a "bondservant" of Christ. It also recalls the honored servants of God in the OT, such as Moses, Joshua, David, and the prophets. **apostle.** Paul's authority is equal to that of the 11 original apostles chosen by Christ (Matt. 10:1–7; Acts 1:24–26; Gal. 1:1), who had seen him after his resurrection (Acts 1:22; 1 Cor. 9:1; 15:7–9).

They established and governed the whole church, under Christ's authority. They had authority to speak and write the words of God, and what they wrote was equal in authority to the OT Scriptures (1 Cor. 14:37; 1 Thess. 2:13). Paul was called to be an apostle when Jesus appeared to him on the Damascus road (Acts 9; 22; 26). **Gospel** means "good news." This includes the call to saving faith and the message of how Jesus transforms all of life and all of history.

**1:2–3** Jesus fulfilled the OT prophecy that a descendant of **David** would rule forever. He is the Messiah (see 2 Sam. 7:12–16; Psalm 132; Isa. 11:1–5).

**1:4** As the eternal **Son of God**, Jesus has reigned forever with the Father and the Holy Spirit. "Son of God" was a Jewish title for the Messiah. Christ's reign as Messiah began when he was raised from the dead **according to the Spirit of holiness** (through the Holy Spirit).

**1:5** Paul's mission is to all humanity. His goal is **to bring about the obedience of faith** (see 16:26). Saving faith results in obedience.

[7] To all those in Rome who are loved by God and called to be saints:

Grace to you and peace from God our Father and the Lord Jesus Christ.

## Longing to Go to Rome

[8] First, I thank my God through Jesus Christ for all of you, because your faith is proclaimed in all the world. [9] For God is my witness, whom I serve with my spirit in the gospel of his Son, that without ceasing I mention you [10] always in my prayers, asking that somehow by God's will I may now at last succeed in coming to you. [11] For I long to see you, that I may impart to you some spiritual gift to strengthen you— [12] that is, that we may be mutually encouraged by each other's faith, both yours and mine. [13] I do not want you to be unaware, brothers,[1] that I have often intended to come to you (but thus far have been prevented), in order that I may reap some harvest among you as well as among the rest of the Gentiles. [14] I am under obligation both to Greeks and to barbarians,[2] both to the wise and to the foolish. [15] So I am eager to preach the gospel to you also who are in Rome.

## The Righteous Shall Live by Faith

[16] For I am not ashamed of the gospel, for it is the power of God for salvation to everyone who believes, to the Jew first and also to the Greek.

[1] Or brothers and sisters. In New Testament usage, depending on the context, the plural Greek word adelphoi (translated "brothers") may refer either to brothers or to brothers and sisters  [2] That is, non-Greeks

**1:7 loved by God and called.** God shows his love by calling his people to himself. All believers are God's **saints**, his "holy ones." **Grace** means God's unmerited favor. **Peace** is not just the absence of conflict. It echoes the OT concept of blessing, in which the person and community are well and whole in all aspects of life.

**1:8 thank.** Paul typically follows the greeting in his letters with a thanksgiving (cf. 1 Cor. 1:1–9; Phil. 1:1–8). He is thankful because the kingdom of God is advancing throughout **all the world**. It is no longer confined to the Jews but has also spread to the Gentiles.

**1:13** Paul neither "planted" nor "watered" the church at Rome (see 1 Cor. 3:6), but he still rejoices in the **harvest** of their increased maturity and obedience.

**1:14** Paul was **under an obligation** to Jesus Christ, who appointed him to be the apostle to the Gentiles. **Greeks.** Those who spoke Greek and adopted Greek culture in the Greco-Roman world. **barbarians.** Those outside of Greek culture.

**1:15 preach the gospel to you also.** The gospel is not just the initial call to saving faith. It is also the call to keep on walking by faith (6:4; 8:4; 2 Cor. 5:17).

**1:16 Jew first.** The Jews have priority in salvation

[17] For in it the righteousness of God is revealed from faith for faith,[1] [a] as it is written, "The righteous shall live by faith."[2]

## God's Wrath on Unrighteousness

[18] For the wrath of God is revealed from heaven against all ungodliness and unrighteousness of men, who by their unrighteousness suppress the truth. [19] For what can be known about God is plain to them, because God has shown it to them. [20] For his invisible attributes, namely, his eternal power and divine nature, have been clearly perceived, ever since the creation of the world,[3] in the things that have been made. So they are without excuse. [21] For although they knew God, they did not honor him as God or give thanks to him, but they became futile in their thinking, and their foolish hearts were darkened. [22] Claiming to be wise, they became fools, [23] and exchanged the glory of the immortal God for images resembling mortal man and birds and animals and creeping things.

[1] Or beginning and ending in faith  [2] Or The one who by faith is righteous shall live  [3] Or clearly perceived from the creation of the world  [a] Hab. 2:4

history because they are God's chosen people. See chs. 9–11. **Greek** refers here to all Gentiles.

**1:17 The righteousness of God** most likely means "righteousness from God." It reflects a right standing before God that is given to people by God (see Phil. 3:9). The phrase likely has this meaning in Rom. 3:21–22 and 2 Cor. 5:21 as well. However, the expression probably also refers to God's righteous moral character. This is seen in his holiness and justice. It is also seen in the way that his act of saving sinners through Christ's death meets the just demand of his holy nature. **From faith for faith** probably means that right standing with God is by faith from start to finish. **shall live by faith.** People receive the gift of salvation by faith. It is also by faith that they live each day. See Hab. 2:4.

**1:18–3:20 God's Righteousness in His Wrath against Sinners.** God's wrath is rightly revealed against all people, since all have sinned (3:23). Paul describes the sinfulness of the Gentiles (1:18–32), and the Jews (2:1–3:8), and of all people, Jew and Gentile alike (3:9–20).

**1:18 The wrath of God** refers to his personal anger against sin. God's anger is his holy response to rejection of his love and law.

**1:19–20 things that have been made.** The entire natural world reveals God through its beauty, complexity, design, and usefulness. **without excuse.** God has given sufficient evidence of his existence and character.

**1:21 they knew God.** All people know God exists. They also know a lot about him, even if they do not have a saving knowledge of him.

**1:22** Even brilliant people who do not honor God miss the whole purpose of life and are therefore fools (see Prov. 1:7).

**1:23** Idolatry is the most basic sin. In addition to the images housed in great temples, Roman families commonly kept images of "house gods" in their homes. People today still devote their lives to, and trust in, many things other than God.

[24] Therefore God gave them up in the lusts of their hearts to impurity, to the dishonoring of their bodies among themselves, [25] because they exchanged the truth about God for a lie and worshiped and served the creature rather than the Creator, who is blessed forever! Amen.

[26] For this reason God gave them up to dishonorable passions. For their women exchanged natural relations for those that are contrary to nature; [27] and the men likewise gave up natural relations with women and were consumed with passion for one another, men committing shameless acts with men and receiving in themselves the due penalty for their error.

[28] And since they did not see fit to acknowledge God, God gave them up to a debased mind to do what ought not to be done. [29] They were filled with all manner of unrighteousness, evil, covetousness, malice. They are full of envy, murder, strife, deceit, maliciousness. They are gossips, [30] slanderers, haters of God, insolent, haughty, boastful, inventors of evil, disobedient to parents, [31] foolish, faithless, heartless, ruthless. [32] Though they know God's righteous decree that those who practice such things deserve to die, they not only do them but give approval to those who practice them.

......................................................................................................................

**1:24** Three times Paul says **God gave them up to sin** (vv. 24, 26, 28). Each time the "giving up" is a reaction to idolatry. The idol worshiper refuses to recognize that God our Maker is the center of all existence. He worships the "creature" rather than the "Creator" (v. 25).

**1:25 exchanged the truth about God for a lie.** All non-Christian religions are based on false ideas about God. They are not just "different paths" to God.

**1:26–27** Not only homosexual acts but also homosexual **passions** or desires are **dishonorable** before God. Just as idolatry is unnatural (contrary to what God intended), so too homosexuality is con-

trary to nature. God made men and women with physical bodies that have a "natural" way of interacting with each other. **Men . . . with men** includes all homosexual relationships, not just those generally considered abusive. **Due penalty** could refer to the sin of homosexuality itself. Or, the "and" in **and receiving** may indicate some additional negative consequences received **in themselves**, that is, some form of spiritual, emotional, or physical disorder.

**1:32** People do not generally sin in innocent ignorance. They **know God's righteous decree** (at least in an instinctive way) that their evildoing deserves punishment.

*God's Righteous Judgment*

2 Therefore you have no excuse, O man, every one of you who judges. For in passing judgment on another you condemn yourself, because you, the judge, practice the very same things. [2] We know that the judgment of God rightly falls on those who practice such things. [3] Do you suppose, O man—you who judge those who practice such things and yet do them yourself—that you will escape the judgment of God? [4] Or do you presume on the riches of his kindness and forbearance and patience, not knowing that God's kindness is meant to lead you to repentance? [5] But because of your hard and impenitent heart you are storing up wrath for yourself on the day of wrath when God's righteous judgment will be revealed.

[6] He will render to each one according to his works: [7] to those who by patience in well-doing seek for glory and honor and immortality, he will give eternal life; [8] but for those who are self-seeking[1] and do not obey the truth, but obey unrighteousness, there will be wrath and fury. [9] There will be tribulation and distress for every human being who does evil, the Jew first and also the Greek, [10] but glory and honor and peace for everyone who does good, the Jew first and also the Greek. [11] For God shows no partiality.

[1] Or *contentious*

---

**2:1–29** Most interpreters say that Paul focuses on the sin of the Jews throughout this chapter. Another view is that the sin of the moral person (whether Jewish or Gentile) who judges others is condemned in vv. 1–16, while Jews alone are condemned in vv. 17–29.

**2:4 Do you presume** is probably addressed to Jews who thought that their covenant relationship with God would save them from final judgment. They thought that **his kindness and forbearance and patience** showed that they were right with him and had no need for Christ. Paul says God's blessings should have led them to repent of their sins.

**2:5** A soft and repentant heart is needed to avoid God's wrath on the **day of wrath**, the final judgment. Such repentance leads a person to trust in Jesus Christ for the forgiveness of sins. Unfortunately, most people are **storing up wrath** for themselves on that final day.

**2:6–11** Paul establishes the principle that God judges **according to . . . works**. In doing so, he shows **no partiality**.

## God's Judgment and the Law

[12] For all who have sinned without the law will also perish without the law, and all who have sinned under the law will be judged by the law. [13] For it is not the hearers of the law who are righteous before God, but the doers of the law who will be justified. [14] For when Gentiles, who do not have the law, by nature do what the law requires, they are a law to themselves, even though they do not have the law. [15] They show that the work of the law is written on their hearts, while their conscience also bears witness, and their conflicting thoughts accuse or even excuse them [16] on that day when, according to my gospel, God judges the secrets of men by Christ Jesus.

[17] But if you call yourself a Jew and rely on the law and boast in God [18] and know his will and approve what is excellent, because you are instructed from the law; [19] and if you are sure that you yourself are a guide to the blind, a light to those who are in darkness, [20] an instructor of the foolish, a teacher of children, having in the law the embodiment of knowledge and truth— [21] you then who teach others, do you not teach yourself? While you preach against stealing, do you steal? [22] You who say that one must not commit adultery, do you commit adultery? You who abhor idols, do you rob temples? [23] You who boast in the law dishonor God by breaking the law. [24] For, [a] as it is written, "The name of God is blasphemed among the Gentiles because of you."

[a] Isa. 52:5

**2:12** All will be judged according to the standard they had. Gentiles will **perish** (face final judgment) because of their sin (see vv. 14–15) even though they are **without the law** (the written laws of the OT). Jews, who possess the law, will be **judged** for their transgressions against it.

**2:14–16** For Gentiles, God's law is **written on their hearts**. Their consciences show what is right or wrong in their behavior. Paul does not imply that the human conscience is always a perfect moral guide (see 1 Cor. 8:7, 10; 10:29). But its existence is enough to make people accountable to God.

**2:16** my gospel. Not Paul's alone, but the gospel that he preaches.

**2:21–24** The Jews fail to practice the law they proclaim. Thus they will face judgment.

**2:22** rob temples. Robbing temples was a common crime in the ancient world because temples contained expensive items that could be sold for profit.

**2:24** Because they violated the law, the Jews were

[25] For circumcision indeed is of value if you obey the law, but if you break the law, your circumcision becomes uncircumcision. [26] So, if a man who is uncircumcised keeps the precepts of the law, will not his uncircumcision be regarded[1] as circumcision? [27] Then he who is physically[2] uncircumcised but keeps the law will condemn you who have the written code[3] and circumcision but break the law. [28] For no one is a Jew who is merely one outwardly, nor is circumcision outward and physical. [29] But a Jew is one inwardly, and circumcision is a matter of the heart, by the Spirit, not by the letter. His praise is not from man but from God.

### God's Righteousness Upheld

3 Then what advantage has the Jew? Or what is the value of circumcision? [2] Much in every way. To begin with, the Jews were entrusted with the oracles of God. [3] What if some were unfaithful? Does their faithlessness nullify the faithfulness of God? [4] By no means! Let God be true though every one were a liar, as it is written,

[1] Or *counted*  [2] Or *is by nature*  [3] Or *the letter*

---

exiled by God. Their military and political defeats dishonored God because they were known as his people. Although the Jews did not face exile in Paul's day, their sins still led Gentiles to dishonor the God they claimed to follow.

**2:25–26** The Jews tended to believe that they would be spared at the last judgment because of their **circumcision** (Gen. 17:9–14; Lev. 12:3). **uncircumcision.** Paul argues, however, that Jews who violate the law are considered by God to be uncircumcised. They are outside the covenant and headed for judgment. Circumcision would be of **value** for salvation if the circumcised would **obey the law** perfectly, but no one can do that. Paul takes up the issue of circumcision again in Rom. 4:9–16.

**2:27** The **written code** refers to OT laws.

**2:28–29** In striking contrast to Jewish beliefs of his day, Paul claims that true Jewishness and genuine circumcision are not ethnic or physical matters. Rather, they are matters **of the heart**. They are the

work of the Holy Spirit. This letter/Spirit contrast compares the old era of redemptive history with the new age begun by Jesus Christ.

**3:1** Now Paul raises the logical question of whether there is any **advantage** or **value** in being an ethnic Jew and being physically circumcised. He probably means "value for salvation."

**3:2** One might expect Paul to answer that there is no advantage in being a Jew (see v. 1). Instead, he claims that the Jews have great advantages, mainly in possessing **the oracles of God**, which refers to the OT Scriptures. On the **Jews** being **entrusted** with the oracles of God, see Deut. 4:8; 5:22–27; Ps. 147:20.

**3:3–4** Even though most Jews were **unfaithful** and refused to trust and obey God, he remains faithful to them. God will fulfill his covenant promises, particularly his promise to save them. Paul does not mean that every single Jew will be saved, though. He discusses God's faithfulness to the Jews more fully in chs. 9–11.

> [a]"That you may be justified in your words,
>
> and prevail when you are judged."

[5] But if our unrighteousness serves to show the righteousness of God, what shall we say? That God is unrighteous to inflict wrath on us? (I speak in a human way.) [6] By no means! For then how could God judge the world? [7] But if through my lie God's truth abounds to his glory, why am I still being condemned as a sinner? [8] And why not do evil that good may come?—as some people slanderously charge us with saying. Their condemnation is just.

## No One Is Righteous

[9] What then? Are we Jews[1] any better off?[2] No, not at all. For we have already charged that all, both Jews and Greeks, are under sin, [10] as it is written:

> [b]"None is righteous, no, not one;
>
> [11]  no one understands;
>
> no one seeks for God.
>
> [12]  All have turned aside; together they have become worthless;
>
> no one does good,
>
> not even one."
>
> [13]  [c]"Their throat is an open grave;
>
> they use their tongues to deceive."

[1] Greek *Are we*  [2] Or *at any disadvantage?*  [a] Ps. 51:4 (Gk.)  [b] Ps. 14:1-3; 53:1-3  [c] Ps. 5:9

**3:5-8** Some of Paul's Jewish opponents claimed that he taught a doctrine of "cheap grace," that is, that God receives more glory when Christians **do evil** and then are forgiven. Paul emphatically denies this but waits until ch. 6 to discuss this charge in more detail.

**3:9 Greeks**. The entire Gentile world in contrast to the Jews.

For an additional resource on v. 9, see p. 114.

**3:10-12** Paul focuses on the sinfulness of every human being, citing Ps. 14:1-3 and perhaps thinking of Eccles. 7:20. **no one does good**. Human beings do some things that seem to be good. But these actions, prior to salvation, are still stained by evil because they are not done for God's glory (Rom. 1:21) and do not come from faith (14:23).

**3:13-14** Paul quotes from Ps. 5:9 and 10:7. The reference to the **grave** highlights either the corruption of the heart or the deadly effects of sin.

<sup>a</sup>"The venom of asps is under their lips."

14      <sup>b</sup>"Their mouth is full of curses and bitterness."

15      <sup>c</sup>"Their feet are swift to shed blood;

16          in their paths are ruin and misery,

17      and the way of peace they have not known."

18          <sup>d</sup>"There is no fear of God before their eyes."

<sup>19</sup> Now we know that whatever the law says it speaks to those who are under the law, so that every mouth may be stopped, and the whole world may be held accountable to God. <sup>20</sup> For by works of the law no human being<sup>1</sup> will be justified in his sight, since through the law comes knowledge of sin.

*The Righteousness of God Through Faith*

<sup>21</sup> But now the righteousness of God has been manifested apart from the law, although the Law and the Prophets bear witness to it— <sup>22</sup> the righteousness of God through faith in Jesus Christ for all who believe. For there is no distinction: <sup>23</sup> for all have sinned and fall short of the glory of God, <sup>24</sup> and are justified by his grace as a gift, through the redemption that

---

<sup>1</sup> Greek *flesh*  <sup>a</sup> Ps. 140:3  <sup>b</sup> Ps. 10:7 (Gk.)  <sup>c</sup> Prov. 1:16; 3:15-17; Isa. 59:7, 8  <sup>d</sup> Ps. 36:1

**3:15-17** Paul draws from Isa. 59:7-8 to show how human history includes murder, war, and disorder.

**3:18** The root cause of sin is failure to **fear** and honor God (Ps. 36:1).

**3:19-20** These verses represent the conclusion of vv. 9-18 and all of 1:18-3:20. All humans, without exception, are sinners.

**3:19 law.** The Mosaic law.

**3:20 Works of the law** means all that the law requires. **Justified** is a legal term meaning "declared righteous."

**3:21-4:25 The Saving Righteousness of God.** Paul now explains that people can have a right standing

with God only through faith in the atoning work of Jesus on the cross.

**3:21** The righteousness of God has been shown **now**, in the period of salvation history that began with Jesus' death and resurrection. On the **righteousness of God**, see note on 1:17. By God's saving acts in Christ, humans may stand in the right before God, the divine judge. **apart from the law.** Righteousness is not based on obeying the law. Yet **the Law and the Prophets bear witness to it.** The OT Scriptures looked forward to salvation through Christ (see 1:2).

**3:24 Justified.** Counted righteous or declared righteous by God (Gal. 2:16). The word **redemption** recalls the exodus and the blood of the Passover lamb (see Exodus 12-15; Eph. 1:7; Col. 1:14).

is in Christ Jesus, [25] whom God put forward as a propitiation by his blood, to be received by faith. This was to show God's righteousness, because in his divine forbearance he had passed over former sins. [26] It was to show his righteousness at the present time, so that he might be just and the justifier of the one who has faith in Jesus.

[27] Then what becomes of our boasting? It is excluded. By what kind of law? By a law of works? No, but by the law of faith. [28] For we hold that one is justified by faith apart from works of the law. [29] Or is God the God of Jews only? Is he not the God of Gentiles also? Yes, of Gentiles also, [30] since God is one—who will justify the circumcised by faith and the uncircumcised through faith. [31] Do we then overthrow the law by this faith? By no means! On the contrary, we uphold the law.

## Abraham Justified by Faith

4 What then shall we say was gained by Abraham, our forefather according to the flesh? [2] For if Abraham was justified by works, he has something to boast about, but not before God. [3] For what does the Scripture say?

---

**3:25** Jesus' blood "propitiated" or satisfied God's wrath (1:18). Thus he could forgive sinners while also maintaining his holiness. Some scholars argue that the word **propitiation** should be translated *expiation* (the wiping away of sin), but the word refers to the satisfaction of God's wrath, turning it from wrath to favor. God's righteous anger needed to be satisfied before sin could be forgiven. God in his love sent his Son to meet the demands of God's holy anger against sin. God's justice was questioned because he had patiently overlooked **former** sins. But Paul says that God knew Christ's death would happen, where the full payment for the guilt of sin would be made.

**3:26** In the cross of Christ, God has shown himself to be **just** (utterly holy, so that the penalty demanded by the law is not removed but is paid by Christ). He is also **the justifier** of all those who trust in Jesus. That is, he provides the means of justification and declares people to be in right standing with himself. Here is the heart of the Christian faith, for at the cross God's justice and love meet.

**3:27** The word **law** in this verse probably means principle, though some think it refers to the OT law.

**3:28** Justification is **by faith** alone, **apart from . . . the law**. It does not depend at all on doing any works of the law.

**3:29–30** Since **God** is the Lord of all, whether **Jews** or **Gentiles**, there can be only one way of justification—by **faith**.

**3:31** Although Paul supports the lasting moral teachings of the law (**uphold**), he knows that some will accuse him of abandoning it (**overthrow**). He will defend himself against such charges in chs. 6–7.

**4:1–25** Abraham, the father of the Jewish people, is presented as a test case for the view that justification is by faith alone.

**4:3** Abraham had a right standing before God by believing, not by doing (Gen. 15:6).

[a]"Abraham believed God, and it was counted to him as righteousness." [4]Now to the one who works, his wages are not counted as a gift but as his due. [5]And to the one who does not work but believes in[1] him who justifies the ungodly, his faith is counted as righteousness, [6]just as David also speaks of the blessing of the one to whom God counts righteousness apart from works:

7      [b]"Blessed are those whose lawless deeds are forgiven,
        and whose sins are covered;

8      blessed is the man against whom the Lord will not count his sin."

[9]Is this blessing then only for the circumcised, or also for the uncircumcised? For we say that faith was counted to Abraham as righteousness. [10]How then was it counted to him? Was it before or after he had been circumcised? It was not after, but before he was circumcised. [11]He received the sign of circumcision as a seal of the righteousness that he had by faith while he was still uncircumcised. The purpose was to make him the father of all who believe without being circumcised, so that righteousness would be counted to them as well, [12]and to make him the father of the circumcised who are not merely circumcised but who also walk in the footsteps of the faith that our father Abraham had before he was circumcised.

### The Promise Realized Through Faith

[13]For the promise to Abraham and his offspring that he would be heir of the world did not come through the law but through the righteousness

[1] Or *but trusts; compare verse 24* [a] Gen. 15:6 (Gk.) [b] Ps. 32:1, 2

**4:6–8** Paul introduces **David** as a second example of righteousness by faith, citing Ps. 32:1–2.

**4:11 sign . . . seal.** Circumcision proved the righteousness by faith that Abraham had before his circumcision.

**4:13–14** The **world** to come is another term for the final salvation that will be given to Abraham and all believers (see Heb. 11:10–16; Revelation 21–22). If the inheritance is gained by observing the **law**, then righteousness is no longer by **faith** but by works.

of faith. [14] For if it is the adherents of the law who are to be the heirs, faith is null and the promise is void. [15] For the law brings wrath, but where there is no law there is no transgression.

[16] That is why it depends on faith, in order that the promise may rest on grace and be guaranteed to all his offspring—not only to the adherent of the law but also to the one who shares the faith of Abraham, who is the father of us all, [17] as it is written, [a] "I have made you the father of many nations"—in the presence of the God in whom he believed, who gives life to the dead and calls into existence the things that do not exist. [18] In hope he believed against hope, that he should become the father of many nations, as he had been told, [b] "So shall your offspring be." [19] He did not weaken in faith when he considered his own body, which was as good as dead (since he was about a hundred years old), or when he considered the barrenness[1] of Sarah's womb. [20] No unbelief made him waver concerning the promise of God, but he grew strong in his faith as he gave glory to God, [21] fully convinced that God was able to do what he had promised. [22] That is why his faith was "counted to him as righteousness." [23] But the words "it was counted to him" were not written for his sake alone, [24] but for ours also. It will be counted to us who believe in him who raised from the dead Jesus our Lord, [25] who was delivered up for our trespasses and raised for our justification.

[1] Greek *deadness*  [a] Gen. 17:5  [b] Gen. 15:5

........................................................................

**4:15 transgression.** The violation of a revealed command. The Jews, who had the written law, had even greater responsibility for their sin. Paul argues elsewhere that sin also exists where no written law is involved; see 2:12, and note on 5:13.

**4:16 Faith** means trusting in another, not in one's own efforts. It corresponds exactly to **grace**, which involves trusting God's gift of unearned favor. **The adherent of the law** refers to the Jewish believer in Christ. **father of us all.** Abraham is the father of all believers, whether Jew or Gentile.

**4:17 many nations.** Genesis 17:5 confirms Abraham's universal fatherhood. **calls into existence the things that do not exist.** If God created the world out of nothing, he could certainly give Sarah a child.

**4:23–24 but for ours also.** In God's plan, Scriptures as far back as Gen. 15:6 apply also to Christians in the new covenant age.

**4:25 raised for our justification.** Both the death and the resurrection of Jesus Christ are necessary for forgiveness of sins and justification. When God raised Christ from the dead, it showed that he

*Peace with God Through Faith*

5 Therefore, since we have been justified by faith, we[1] have peace with God through our Lord Jesus Christ. [2] Through him we have also obtained access by faith[2] into this grace in which we stand, and we[3] rejoice[4] in hope of the glory of God. [3] Not only that, but we rejoice in our sufferings, knowing that suffering produces endurance, [4] and endurance produces character, and character produces hope, [5] and hope does not put us to shame, because God's love has been poured into our hearts through the Holy Spirit who has been given to us.

[6] For while we were still weak, at the right time Christ died for the ungodly. [7] For one will scarcely die for a righteous person—though perhaps for a good person one would dare even to die— [8] but God shows his love for us in that while we were still sinners, Christ died for us. [9] Since, therefore, we have now been justified by his blood, much more shall we be saved by him from the wrath of God. [10] For if while we were enemies we were reconciled to God by the death of his Son, much more, now that we are reconciled, shall

[1] Some manuscripts *let us*   [2] Some manuscripts omit *by faith*   [3] Or *let us; also verse 3*   [4] Or *boast; also verses 3, 11*

accepted Christ's suffering and death as full payment for sin. At the cross, God had directed his wrath against Christ, but now, in the resurrection, God showed his favor to Christ and to all who would believe in him. This can be true because all who believe in Christ are united with him (see 6:6, 8–11; Eph. 2:6; Col. 2:12; 3:1).

**5:1–8:39 Hope as a Result of Righteousness by Faith.** Believers in Christ, who are righteous in God's sight, have a sure hope of future glory and life eternal.

**5:1** Through **faith** in Christ, Christians have been **justified** and declared righteous by God once for all. They no longer need to live in fear of God's wrath and judgment. Rather, they enjoy **peace with God**.

**5:2** grace in which we stand. The believers' secure position as a result of their justification. hope of the glory of God. The promise that Christians will be glorified and perfected at the last day.

**5:5** hope does not put us to shame. Followers of Christ have no reason to fear humiliation on the judgment day, for they now belong to God.

**5:6** In this and the following verses, Paul shows how the believer's subjective experience of God's love (v. 5) is firmly based on the objective work of Christ on the cross. **Weak** here refers to lack of moral strength and is another way to describe those who are **ungodly**.

**5:9** Christians are **justified** (declared right before God) because of Christ's **blood** poured out at the cross. Therefore, they can know that they will be saved from God's **wrath** on the day of judgment.

**5:10** As in v. 9, Paul argues from the greater to the lesser. Since Christians are now **reconciled** to God through Christ's death, they can be assured that they will be **saved** on the day to come. Here "saved" includes initial justification, completed sanctification, glorification, and future rewards. Salvation is based on **his life**, that is, Christ's resurrection (see 4:25; 6:1–23).

we be saved by his life. [11] More than that, we also rejoice in God through our Lord Jesus Christ, through whom we have now received reconciliation.

## Death in Adam, Life in Christ

[12] Therefore, just as sin came into the world through one man, and death through sin, and so death spread to all men[1] because all sinned— [13] for sin indeed was in the world before the law was given, but sin is not counted where there is no law. [14] Yet death reigned from Adam to Moses, even over those whose sinning was not like the transgression of Adam, who was a type of the one who was to come.

[15] But the free gift is not like the trespass. For if many died through one man's trespass, much more have the grace of God and the free gift by the grace of that one man Jesus Christ abounded for many. [16] And the free gift is not like the result of that one man's sin. For the judgment following one

[1] The Greek word *anthropoi* refers here to both men and women; also twice in verse 18

**5:12–21** Adam brought sin and death into the world, but those who have believed in Christ have hope. Christ has reversed the consequences of Adam's sin and has given his own life and righteousness to secure their eternal glory. The extended comparison between Adam and Christ shows that Paul considered Adam a historical person.

**5:12 Sin came into the world through one man,** namely, Adam (v. 14; see Gen. 3:17–19; 1 Cor. 15:21–22). **and death through sin.** Death is "the last enemy" (1 Cor. 15:26; see 15:54) and will be conquered forever at Christ's return (Rev. 21:4). "Death" in these verses most likely includes both physical and spiritual death. Paul often connects the two. **And so death spread to all men** probably means "and in this way death spread to all men." **Because all sinned** probably means that all people participated in Adam's sin because he represented all who would descend from him (just as Christ's obedience counts for all his followers; Rom. 5:15–19). Another interpretation is that all people have sinned individually as a result of being born into the world spiritually dead. The word translated "men" can mean either males or people of both sexes, depending on the context. It is translated "men" here (and in v. 18) to show the connection with "man," referring to Christ.

**5:13 sin is not counted where there is no law.** Paul does not mean that people are guiltless without the law (see 2:12). Those without the written law are still judged by God (see Genesis 6–9; 11:1–9).

**5:14** Those who did not live under the law were still judged for their sin, and therefore they died. Still, their **sinning was not like the transgression of Adam:** Adam violated a commandment specifically given to him by God. Adam is a **type** (that is, a model or pattern) of Christ. Both Adam and Christ are covenantal heads of the human race. All people are either "in Adam" or "in Christ" (see 1 Cor. 15:22). All are "in Adam" by physical birth, while only those who have placed their faith in Christ are "in" him.

**5:15** Paul contrasts the consequences of the work of Adam and of Christ five times in the next five verses. This shows their roles as covenantal heads of the people they represent. Paul clearly teaches "original sin," the fact that all people inherit a sinful nature because of Adam's sin. Paul probably is also teaching that all people are in fact guilty before God because of Adam's sin. **Many** (that is, all human beings excluding Christ) **died**. Death begins with spiritual separation from God and ends in physical death.

**5:16** The **one trespass** of Adam resulted in the **condemnation** of all. But Christ overcame sin; therefore all who belong to him enjoy **justification**.

trespass brought condemnation, but the free gift following many trespasses brought justification. **¹⁷** For if, because of one man's trespass, death reigned through that one man, much more will those who receive the abundance of grace and the free gift of righteousness reign in life through the one man Jesus Christ.

**¹⁸** Therefore, as one trespass¹ led to condemnation for all men, so one act of righteousness² leads to justification and life for all men. **¹⁹** For as by the one man's disobedience the many were made sinners, so by the one man's obedience the many will be made righteous. **²⁰** Now the law came in to increase the trespass, but where sin increased, grace abounded all the more, **²¹** so that, as sin reigned in death, grace also might reign through righteousness leading to eternal life through Jesus Christ our Lord.

### Dead to Sin, Alive to God

**6** What shall we say then? Are we to continue in sin that grace may abound? **²** By no means! How can we who died to sin still live in it? **³** Do you not know that all of us who have been baptized into Christ Jesus were baptized into

¹ Or *the trespass of one* ² Or *the act of righteousness of one*

**5:17** Death ruled the human race due to Adam's sin, but Christians now stand in eternal life as rulers because of Christ's work.

**5:18 for all men.** Based on these verses, some interpreters have argued that all people will be saved. But Paul makes it plain that only those who "receive" God's gift belong to Christ (v. 17; see also 1:16–5:11). The wording "as . . . so" shows that Paul's focus is not on *how many* will be saved but on the *method* of either sin or righteousness being passed from the representative leader to the whole group. **men.** See note on 5:12.

**5:19** Because of Adam's disobedience, all people **were made** (caused to be) **sinners.** When Adam (mankind's representative) sinned, God viewed the whole human race as guilty sinners. All are born with a sinful nature because of Adam's sin.

**5:20** The typical Jewish view in Paul's day was that God gave the law in order to reduce the human impulse to sin. But Paul claims that the law was given **to increase the trespass.** That is, once people had written laws from God, they were not just committing "sins" against God's law as it was ingrained in their conscience (see note on 2:14–16); rather, they were willfully "trespassing" against his written word. Amid this increasing sin, however, the **grace** revealed through Christ **abounded all the more.**

**6:1–23** The law does not and cannot conquer sin, but the grace given to followers of Christ triumphs over sin and death.

**6:1** Paul is likely responding to a question posed regularly by his Jewish opponents. They argued that his gospel led people to **continue in sin.**

**6:3** Christians died to sin when they were **baptized into Christ.** Paul is not arguing that baptism destroys the power of sin. Baptism is an outward, physical symbol of the inward, spiritual conversion of Christians.

his death? [4] We were buried therefore with him by baptism into death, in order that, just as Christ was raised from the dead by the glory of the Father, we too might walk in newness of life.

[5] For if we have been united with him in a death like his, we shall certainly be united with him in a resurrection like his. [6] We know that our old self[1] was crucified with him in order that the body of sin might be brought to nothing, so that we would no longer be enslaved to sin. [7] For one who has died has been set free[2] from sin. [8] Now if we have died with Christ, we believe that we will also live with him. [9] We know that Christ, being raised from the dead, will never die again; death no longer has dominion over him. [10] For the death he died he died to sin, once for all, but the life he lives he lives to God. [11] So you also must consider yourselves dead to sin and alive to God in Christ Jesus.

[12] Let not sin therefore reign in your mortal body, to make you obey its passions. [13] Do not present your members to sin as instruments for unrighteousness, but present yourselves to God as those who have been brought from death to life, and your members to God as instruments for righteousness. [14] For sin will have no dominion over you, since you are not under law but under grace.

[1] Greek man  [2] Greek has been justified

**6:4** In the early church, baptism was probably by immersion. Baptism pictures being **buried** with Christ (going under the water) and being **raised** to new life with Christ (coming up from the water). This symbolizes union with, and incorporation into, Christ by the action of the Holy Spirit. Believers now have the power to live in **newness** of life.

**6:6** The power of sin has been broken in those who believe. Their **old self** (literally, "old man," meaning who they were in Adam) **was crucified** and put to death with Christ. **Body of sin** refers to the ruling power of sin that people willingly accept. Paul does not argue that Christians do not sin at all, but he does say that they are no longer **enslaved to sin**. The normal pattern of life for Christians should be

progressive growth in maturity and obedience to God's moral law.

**6:7 One who has died** means one who has died with Christ.

**6:10 died to sin.** Jesus died because he took sin upon himself. His resurrection demonstrates that he has defeated both sin and death.

**6:11 dead to sin.** Dead to the continual love for and ruling power of sin (see note on v. 6).

**6:12–13** Tension occurs here between what God has already accomplished and his people's responsibility to obey. They are still tempted by desires to sin and must not let those desires gain control.

**6:14 sin will have no dominion over you.** This is not

*Slaves to Righteousness*

[15] What then? Are we to sin because we are not under law but under grace? By no means! [16] Do you not know that if you present yourselves to anyone as obedient slaves,[1] you are slaves of the one whom you obey, either of sin, which leads to death, or of obedience, which leads to righteousness? [17] But thanks be to God, that you who were once slaves of sin have become obedient from the heart to the standard of teaching to which you were committed, [18] and, having been set free from sin, have become slaves of righteousness. [19] I am speaking in human terms, because of your natural limitations. For just as you once presented your members as slaves to impurity and to lawlessness leading to more lawlessness, so now present your members as slaves to righteousness leading to sanctification.

[20] For when you were slaves of sin, you were free in regard to righteousness. [21] But what fruit were you getting at that time from the things of which you are now ashamed? For the end of those things is death. [22] But now that you have been set free from sin and have become slaves of God, the fruit you get leads to sanctification and its end, eternal life. [23] For the wages of sin is death, but the free gift of God is eternal life in Christ Jesus our Lord.

[1] For the contextual rendering of the Greek word *doulos*, see Preface; twice in this verse; also verses 17, 19 (twice), 20

a command but a promise that sin will not defeat Christians. **under grace.** The new covenant in Christ (see 3:24; 4:16; 5:2, 15–21).

**6:16** Giving in to sin leads to becoming **obedient slaves** to sin. This eventually **leads to death.** This does not mean that genuine believers can lose their salvation. It means that sinning leads them away from full enjoyment of life with Christ. However, people who do give themselves utterly to sin will die, that is, they will face eternal punishment.

**6:20–21** Both physical and spiritual **death** are probably meant here.

**6:23** Wages implies that the punishment for sin is what one has earned and deserves. **Free gift** is the opposite of something one deserves. This fits Paul's earlier emphasis on justification by grace alone (God's unmerited favor; see note on 4:16),

*Released from the Law*

7 Or do you not know, brothers[1]—for I am speaking to those who know the law—that the law is binding on a person only as long as he lives? [2] For a married woman is bound by law to her husband while he lives, but if her husband dies she is released from the law of marriage.[2] [3] Accordingly, she will be called an adulteress if she lives with another man while her husband is alive. But if her husband dies, she is free from that law, and if she marries another man she is not an adulteress.

[4] Likewise, my brothers, you also have died to the law through the body of Christ, so that you may belong to another, to him who has been raised from the dead, in order that we may bear fruit for God. [5] For while we were living in the flesh, our sinful passions, aroused by the law, were at work in our members to bear fruit for death. [6] But now we are released from the law, having died to that which held us captive, so that we serve in the new way of the Spirit and not in the old way of the written code.[3]

*The Law and Sin*

[7] What then shall we say? That the law is sin? By no means! Yet if it had not been for the law, I would not have known sin. For I would not have

[1] Or brothers and sisters; also verse 4   [2] Greek law concerning the husband   [3] Greek of the letter

............................................................................

through faith alone (trusting in Christ for justification; see 1:17; 3:21–4:25).

**7:1–3** In this entire chapter, **law** refers to the Mosaic law given at Mount Sinai. **Those who know the law** includes both Jews and Gentiles who are familiar with the OT. Verse 1 introduces the principle that the law applies only to living people. In vv. 2–3, Paul applies that principle to marriage.

**7:4** Whereas the *husband* dies in the illustration in vv. 2–3, here *believers* die to the law through the death of *Christ*. The comparison does not match perfectly, but the application is clear.

**7:5** Flesh here stands for the old "Adam"—the unbelieving former life of those who now believe.

The law led to spiritual and physical **death** (see 6:23) because rebellious people broke it and suffered the consequences.

**7:6 But now** represents the new era of redemptive history. Christians now enjoy new life in the Spirit.

**7:7–25** The claim that the Mosaic law produced sin and death raises the question, Is the law itself sinful? Paul explains that the law itself is good and that the fault lies with sin. The "I" in these verses seems to be Paul himself (see note on vv. 13–25).

**7:7** The law defines sin. People ignore God's commands in order to indulge their independence. This principle is illustrated from the tenth commandment (Ex. 20:17).

known what it is to covet if [a] the law had not said, "You shall not covet." [8] But sin, seizing an opportunity through the commandment, produced in me all kinds of covetousness. For apart from the law, sin lies dead. [9] I was once alive apart from the law, but when the commandment came, sin came alive and I died. [10] The very commandment that promised life proved to be death to me. [11] For sin, seizing an opportunity through the commandment, deceived me and through it killed me. [12] So the law is holy, and the commandment is holy and righteous and good.

[13] Did that which is good, then, bring death to me? By no means! It was sin, producing death in me through what is good, in order that sin might be shown to be sin, and through the commandment might become sinful beyond measure. [14] For we know that the law is spiritual, but I am of the flesh, sold under sin. [15] For I do not understand my own actions. For I do not do what I want, but I do the very thing I hate. [16] Now if I do what I do not want, I agree with the law, that it is good. [17] So now it is no longer I who do it, but sin that dwells within me. [18] For I know that nothing good dwells in me, that is, in my flesh. For I have the desire to do what is right, but not

[a] Ex. 20:17; Deut. 5:21

**7:8** The prohibition against coveting increased the desire for what was forbidden. Without such prohibitions, **sin lies dead**—it is still present, but not in a powerful way.

**7:13–25** Even if the law is not sin (vv. 7–12), is the good law responsible for death? Paul argues that the fault lies with sin, not with the law. Through the law, sin is revealed in all its horror, while the law is shown to be good. There has been much debate as to whether Paul is describing believers or unbelievers. Although good arguments are given by both sides, the most widely held view is that Paul is referring to *believers*. Advocates of both positions agree that Christians struggle with sin their whole lives (see Gal. 5:17; 1 John 1:8–9). They also agree that Christians can and should grow in sanctification throughout their lives by the power of the Holy Spirit (Rom. 8:2, 4, 9, 13–14). Those who think Paul is describing believers usually see this passage as describing both Paul's own experience and the experience of Christians generally. This view is that Christians are free from the condemnation of the law, but sin continues to dwell within them. They should understand how far they fall short of God's absolute standard of righteousness. Thus Paul cries out, "Wretched man that I am! Who will deliver me from this body of death?" (7:24). The answer follows immediately: the one who *has* delivered Christians once for all (see 4:2–25; 5:2, 9) and who *will* deliver them day by day is "Jesus Christ our Lord!" (7:25). This reflects the ongoing tension between the "already" aspect of salvation (believers *have been* saved) and the "not yet" aspect (believers *will be* saved at the return of Christ).

**7:17** Paul emphasizes the power of sin.

the ability to carry it out. [19] For I do not do the good I want, but the evil I

do not want is what I keep on doing. [20] Now if I do what I do not want, it is

no longer I who do it, but sin that dwells within me.

[21] So I find it to be a law that when I want to do right, evil lies close at

hand. [22] For I delight in the law of God, in my inner being, [23] but I see in my

members another law waging war against the law of my mind and making

me captive to the law of sin that dwells in my members. [24] Wretched man

that I am! Who will deliver me from this body of death? [25] Thanks be to God

through Jesus Christ our Lord! So then, I myself serve the law of God with

my mind, but with my flesh I serve the law of sin.

## Life in the Spirit

**8** There is therefore now no condemnation for those who are in Christ

Jesus.[1] [2] For the law of the Spirit of life has set you[2] free in Christ Jesus from

the law of sin and death. [3] For God has done what the law, weakened by the

flesh, could not do. By sending his own Son in the likeness of sinful flesh

and for sin,[3] he condemned sin in the flesh, [4] in order that the righteous

---

[1] Some manuscripts add *who walk not according to the flesh (but according to the Spirit)* [2] Some manuscripts *me* [3] Or *and as a sin offering*

---

**7:21–23** The meaning of "law" in these verses has been debated. Some think every use of the word refers to the Mosaic law. Most argue that in vv. 21 and 23 the term means "principle." All agree that the Mosaic law is in view in v. 22. The Greek word used here can have either meaning.

**7:24–25** Who will deliver me? The living presence of **Jesus Christ** is the answer to the problem of sin.

**8:1–17** Paul celebrates the new life of the Spirit that Christians enjoy as a result of Christ's saving work.

**8:1 therefore.** Paul summarizes and concludes his preceding argument (see especially 7:23–25 and 3:21–5:21). **Now** matches the "now" in 7:6. Christ began a new era of redemptive history for those who are "now" in right standing before God because of Christ. **No condemnation** echoes 5:1 ("Therefore . . . we have peace with God"). There is "no condemnation" for the Christian because Jesus

has paid the penalty for sin through his death on the cross (8:2–3).

**8:2** Sin has no dominant power in believers' lives. This work of the Holy Spirit is evidence that believers are in Christ. **Law** in both instances means "principle."

**8:3** The law (here, the Mosaic law) could not solve humanity's problem because sin uses the law for its own purposes (see ch. 7). God sent his Son as a sacrifice **for sin** (a sin offering). Jesus paid the full penalty for sin by his sacrifice (**condemned sin**). **in the likeness of sinful flesh.** Jesus became fully human, even though he was sinless. **In the flesh** refers to Christ's body.

**8:4 righteous requirement of the law . . . fulfilled.** This could mean the requirement is fulfilled in the new life that Christians live on the basis of Christ's work. It could also mean Christ's death paid the full penalty of the law.

requirement of the law might be fulfilled in us, who walk not according to the flesh but according to the Spirit. [5] For those who live according to the flesh set their minds on the things of the flesh, but those who live according to the Spirit set their minds on the things of the Spirit. [6] For to set the mind on the flesh is death, but to set the mind on the Spirit is life and peace. [7] For the mind that is set on the flesh is hostile to God, for it does not submit to God's law; indeed, it cannot. [8] Those who are in the flesh cannot please God.

[9] You, however, are not in the flesh but in the Spirit, if in fact the Spirit of God dwells in you. Anyone who does not have the Spirit of Christ does not belong to him. [10] But if Christ is in you, although the body is dead because of sin, the Spirit is life because of righteousness. [11] If the Spirit of him who raised Jesus from the dead dwells in you, he who raised Christ Jesus[1] from the dead will also give life to your mortal bodies through his Spirit who dwells in you.

### Heirs with Christ

[12] So then, brothers,[2] we are debtors, not to the flesh, to live according to the flesh. [13] For if you live according to the flesh you will die, but if by the Spirit you put to death the deeds of the body, you will live. [14] For all who are led by the Spirit of God are sons[3] of God. [15] For you did not receive

[1] Some manuscripts lack *Jesus*  [2] Or *brothers and sisters*; also verse 29  [3] See discussion on "sons" in the Preface

**8:6** To set the mind on the flesh means to constantly desire the things that express fallen, sinful human nature.

**8:8** Because unbelievers (**those who are in the flesh**) are captured by sin and unable to do what God commands, they fail to please God.

**8:9** Paul alternates between **the Spirit of God** and **the Spirit of Christ** here, showing that Christ and God share the same status.

**8:10** The previous verse speaks of the Spirit's indwelling, but here Paul describes Christ's dwelling in Christians. This does not mean that there is

no difference between Christ and the Spirit. It does suggest that Christ and the Spirit are both fully God, and they work together. The presence of the Spirit within believers testifies to the new life they enjoy because Christ's righteousness is now theirs.

**8:13** God and believers each have a role in sanctification. It must occur **by the Spirit** and his power, but **you put to death** shows that one must take an active role in battling sinful habits.

**8:15** Christians are no longer slaves to sin. They are adopted as sons into God's family. The Spirit assures them that God is their father. **Abba** is

the spirit of slavery to fall back into fear, but you have received the Spirit

of adoption as sons, by whom we cry, "Abba! Father!" [16] The Spirit himself

bears witness with our spirit that we are children of God, [17] and if children,

then heirs—heirs of God and fellow heirs with Christ, provided we suffer

with him in order that we may also be glorified with him.

### Future Glory

[18] For I consider that the sufferings of this present time are not worth

comparing with the glory that is to be revealed to us. [19] For the creation waits

with eager longing for the revealing of the sons of God. [20] For the creation

was subjected to futility, not willingly, but because of him who subjected

it, in hope [21] that the creation itself will be set free from its bondage to cor-

ruption and obtain the freedom of the glory of the children of God. [22] For

we know that the whole creation has been groaning together in the pains

of childbirth until now. [23] And not only the creation, but we ourselves,

who have the firstfruits of the Spirit, groan inwardly as we wait eagerly

for adoption as sons, the redemption of our bodies. [24] For in this hope we

were saved. Now hope that is seen is not hope. For who hopes for what he

sees? [25] But if we hope for what we do not see, we wait for it with patience.

---

Aramaic for Father. Paul's use of the term likely comes from Jesus' addressing God in this way (Mark 14:36).

**8:17** A willingness to follow Christ in suffering is another sign of being God's children.

**8:18–39** Paul began this major section of the letter (5:1–8:39) by emphasizing the final hope of believers (5:1–11), and now he concludes with the same emphasis.

**8:18** The ultimate glory that Christians will receive is so great that the **sufferings of this present time** are insignificant in comparison (see 2 Cor. 4:17). Believers look forward to the resurrection of the body (1 Thess. 4:13–18) and to the new heaven and new earth (Rev. 21:1–22:5; see Isa. 65:17).

**8:20–21** When Adam sinned, the created world was also **subjected to futility**. One thinks of the thorns and thistles that accompany work on the land (Gen. 3:17–19) and the pain in childbirth for women (Gen. 3:16). The original **creation** (Genesis 1–2) did not have these things. On the last day, creation will be freed from the effects of sin. It will be far more beautiful, productive, and easy to live in than one can ever imagine.

**8:22** Again **creation** is personified (see v. 19). It longs for the day when salvation will be completed.

**8:23** Christians already have **the firstfruits of the Spirit**. But they still await the day of their final adoption, when their bodies, fully redeemed, are raised from the dead.

[26] Likewise the Spirit helps us in our weakness. For we do not know what to pray for as we ought, but the Spirit himself intercedes for us with groanings too deep for words. [27] And he who searches hearts knows what is the mind of the Spirit, because[1] the Spirit intercedes for the saints according to the will of God. [28] And we know that for those who love God all things work together for good,[2] for those who are called according to his purpose. [29] For those whom he foreknew he also predestined to be conformed to the image of his Son, in order that he might be the firstborn among many brothers. [30] And those whom he predestined he also called, and those whom he called he also justified, and those whom he justified he also glorified.

## God's Everlasting Love

[31] What then shall we say to these things? If God is for us, who can be[3] against us? [32] He who did not spare his own Son but gave him up for us all, how will he not also with him graciously give us all things? [33] Who shall bring any charge against God's elect? It is God who justifies. [34] Who is to condemn? Christ Jesus is the one who died—more than that, who was

---

[1] Or that   [2] Some manuscripts *God works all things together for good*, or *God works in all things for the good*   [3] Or *who is*

**8:26 Groanings too deep for words** (see v. 23) refers to the believers' sense of the Spirit's intercession for them before God.

**8:28 Good** in this context means being like Christ (v. 29), enjoying closer fellowship with God, bearing good fruit for the kingdom, and final glorification (v. 30). It does not mean earthly pleasures.

**8:29** God has always been doing good for his people. **foreknew**. In the OT, the word "know" emphasizes God's special choice of his people (e.g., Gen. 18:19). See Rom. 11:2, where "foreknew" contrasts with "rejected," emphasizing God's choosing his people. God also **predestined** (that is, predetermined) that those whom he chose beforehand would become like Christ.

**8:30** Those **predestined** by God are also **called** to faith through the gospel (see 2 Thess. 2:14) and **justified** (declared to be right in God's sight). Not

all who are invited to believe are actually justified. Thus the "calling" here must refer to an effective call that creates the faith necessary for justification (Rom. 5:1). All those who are justified will also be **glorified** (receive resurrection bodies) on the last day. Paul speaks of glorification as if it were already completed, since God will certainly finish the good work he started (see Phil. 1:6).

**8:33** Satan, their enemies, or even their own consciences may bring charges against **God's elect**. But God declares them justified.

**8:34 Who is to condemn?** The question in v. 33 is repeated. Christians will never be condemned, for (1) Christ died for them and paid the full penalty for their sin; (2) he was raised, showing that his death removed sin; (3) he now is seated at God's right hand (Ps. 110:1); and (4) he intercedes for his people on the basis of his shed blood.

raised—who is at the right hand of God, who indeed is interceding for us.[1] [35] Who shall separate us from the love of Christ? Shall tribulation, or distress, or persecution, or famine, or nakedness, or danger, or sword? [36] As it is written,

> [a]"For your sake we are being killed all the day long;
>     we are regarded as sheep to be slaughtered."

[37] No, in all these things we are more than conquerors through him who loved us. [38] For I am sure that neither death nor life, nor angels nor rulers, nor things present nor things to come, nor powers, [39] nor height nor depth, nor anything else in all creation, will be able to separate us from the love of God in Christ Jesus our Lord.

## God's Sovereign Choice

9 I am speaking the truth in Christ—I am not lying; my conscience bears me witness in the Holy Spirit— [2] that I have great sorrow and unceasing anguish in my heart. [3] For I could wish that I myself were accursed and cut off from Christ for the sake of my brothers,[2] my kinsmen according to the flesh. [4] They are Israelites, and to them belong the

---

[1] Or Is it Christ Jesus who died . . . for us?  [2] Or brothers and sisters  [a] Ps. 44:22

---

**8:38–39 rulers, powers.** Probably angelic and demonic authorities.

**9:1–11:36 God's Righteousness to Israel and to the Gentiles.** Paul has made it clear that God's saving promises have been fulfilled for the Gentiles. He now asks whether the promises God made to ethnic Israel will be fulfilled. If his promises to the Jews remain unfulfilled, how can Gentile Christians be sure that he will fulfill for them all the great promises in ch. 8? Paul answers that God is faithful to his saving promises to Israel (9:6) and that he will ultimately save his people (11:26).

**9:1–29** God's saving promises to Israel are irrevoca-ble since they are based upon his word of promise and his electing grace.

**9:1–3** Paul suffers great **anguish** because his Jewish kinsmen are unsaved (see also 10:1). Indeed, if it were possible, Paul might almost choose to be **accursed** (to suffer punishment in hell) so that his fellow Jews would be saved (see Moses in Ex. 32:30–32).

**9:4** Israel had great privileges. The **Israelites** became God's adopted people when God saved them from Egypt. **Glory** here probably refers to the glory of God in the tabernacle and temple. Israel received the **covenants** in which the Lord promised to save them. God gave his people his **law** at Mount Sinai.

adoption, the glory, the covenants, the giving of the law, the worship, and the promises. [5] To them belong the patriarchs, and from their race, according to the flesh, is the Christ, who is God over all, blessed forever. Amen.

[6] But it is not as though the word of God has failed. For not all who are descended from Israel belong to Israel, [7] and not all are children of Abraham because they are his offspring, but [a] "Through Isaac shall your offspring be named." [8] This means that it is not the children of the flesh who are the children of God, but the children of the promise are counted as offspring. [9] For this is what the promise said: [b] "About this time next year I will return, and Sarah shall have a son." [10] And not only so, but also when Rebekah had conceived children by one man, our forefather Isaac, [11] though they were not yet born and had done nothing either good or bad—in order that God's purpose of election might continue, not because of works but because of him who calls— [12] she was told, [c] "The older will serve the younger." [13] As it is written, [d] "Jacob I loved, but Esau I hated."

[14] What shall we say then? Is there injustice on God's part? By no means! [15] For he says to Moses, [e] "I will have mercy on whom I have mercy, and I will have compassion on whom I have compassion." [16] So then it

[a] Gen. 21:12 [b] Gen. 18:10, 14 [c] Gen. 25:23 [d] Mal. 1:2, 3 [e] Ex. 33:19

He directed their **worship** in the Mosaic law, and he gave them his saving **promises**.

**9:5** The **patriarchs** (Abraham, Isaac, and Jacob) come from Israel. Most important, Jesus the Christ is a man from the Jewish people. He is also fully **God**, and to be praised as such.

**9:6–7** Though many Jews have failed to believe, God's promise to them has not failed. It was never true that *all* of the physical **children of Abraham** were part of the people of God. Genesis 21:12 teaches that the line of promise is traced **through Isaac**, not Ishmael.

**9:9–10** The promise (Gen. 18:10, 14) was not given to Hagar (Genesis 16), but specifically to Sarah and her offspring. The birth of Esau and Jacob is further evidence that God did not promise that every person of Jewish descent would be saved. They had the same parents, yet God chose Jacob and not Esau.

**9:11–13** God did not choose Jacob on the basis of anything in Jacob or Esau's life. He did so to fulfill his **purpose of election**. For the OT background to "election," see Gen. 18:10; Ex. 33:19; Mal. 1:2–3. See also Eph. 1:3–6.

**9:14–16** God is just in choosing one over the other because *no one* deserves to be saved (see 3:23). The salvation of anyone at all is due to God's **mercy** alone, as the words taken from Ex. 33:19 affirm.

depends not on human will or exertion,[1] but on God, who has mercy. [17] For the Scripture says to Pharaoh, [a] "For this very purpose I have raised you up, that I might show my power in you, and that my name might be proclaimed in all the earth." [18] So then he has mercy on whomever he wills, and he hardens whomever he wills.

[19] You will say to me then, "Why does he still find fault? For who can resist his will?" [20] But who are you, O man, to answer back to God? Will what is molded say to its molder, "Why have you made me like this?" [21] Has the potter no right over the clay, to make out of the same lump one vessel for honorable use and another for dishonorable use? [22] What if God, desiring to show his wrath and to make known his power, has endured with much patience vessels of wrath prepared for destruction, [23] in order to make known the riches of his glory for vessels of mercy, which he has prepared beforehand for glory— [24] even us whom he has called, not from the Jews only but also from the Gentiles? [25] As indeed he says in Hosea,

[b] "Those who were not my people I will call 'my people,'

and her who was not beloved I will call 'beloved.'"

[1] Greek *not of him who wills or runs*  [a] Ex. 9:16  [b] Hos. 2:23

---

**9:17** Paul quotes Ex. 9:16 to show that God is sovereign over evil as well as good. Even the wrath of man praises God (Ps. 76:10). For example, God installed **Pharaoh** as ruler and hardened his heart so that God's own saving power and glorious name would be spread throughout the whole world.

**9:19 who can resist his will?** If salvation ultimately depends upon God, and he either has mercy on or hardens whomever he pleases, then how can he charge anyone with guilt?

**9:20–21** Paul does not resolve the problem presented in v. 19 on the basis of human free will. Rather, he insists that human beings should not rebelliously question God's ways. Like a **potter** (see Jer. 18:1–6), God has the right to do what he wishes

with his creation. The **honorable** and **dishonorable** vessels represent those who are saved and those who are not saved. Paul affirms that humans are guilty for their sin, but he offers no explanation as to how this fits with divine sovereignty. He insists that God controls all that happens (see Eph. 1:11). God does not sin, and he is not morally responsible for sin.

**9:22–23** The salvation of any person is due to the marvelous grace and love of God.

**9:25–26** Paul quotes Hos. 2:23 and 1:10 to illustrate God's amazing grace. Those who **are not my people ... will be called "sons of the living God."** In calling the Gentiles to salvation, God calls sinful people to himself. He did the same with Israel.

**26**      [a] "And in the very place where it was said to them, 'You are not

my people,'

there they will be called 'sons of the living God.'"

**27** And Isaiah cries out concerning Israel: [b] "Though the number of the

sons of Israel[1] be as the sand of the sea, only a remnant of them will be saved,

**28** for the Lord will carry out his sentence upon the earth fully and without

delay." **29** And as Isaiah predicted,

[c] "If the Lord of hosts had not left us offspring,

we would have been like Sodom

and become like Gomorrah."

### Israel's Unbelief

**30** What shall we say, then? That Gentiles who did not pursue righteousness

have attained it, that is, a righteousness that is by faith; **31** but that Israel who

pursued a law that would lead to righteousness[2] did not succeed in reaching

that law. **32** Why? Because they did not pursue it by faith, but as if it were based

on works. They have stumbled over the stumbling stone, **33** as it is written,

[d] "Behold, I am laying in Zion a stone of stumbling, and a rock

of offense;

and whoever believes in him will not be put to shame."

[1] Or *children of Israel*  [2] Greek *a law of righteousness*  a Hos. 1:10  b Isa. 10:22, 23  c Isa. 1:9  d Isa. 28:16

**9:27-29** Isaiah 10:22-23 notes that only some of Israel would be saved. Most of **Israel** was judged. Only **a remnant** experienced salvation. Indeed, as Isa. 1:9 says, Israel deserved to be wiped out like Sodom and Gomorrah, but God had mercy and spared some.

**9:30-11:10** God's sovereignty is compatible with human responsibility. Israel should have believed the gospel and trusted in Christ, but the majority refused to do so. Still, God's saving promises will be fulfilled.

**9:32** Following the law to try to establish righteousness led Israel to stumble over the **stone** (Christ). If obeying the law can save them, they see no need to believe in Christ.

**9:33 stumbling**. See Isa. 28:16. Those who trust in

10 Brothers,[1] my heart's desire and prayer to God for them is that they may be saved. [2] For I bear them witness that they have a zeal for God, but not according to knowledge. [3] For, being ignorant of the righteousness of God, and seeking to establish their own, they did not submit to God's righteousness. [4] For Christ is the end of the law for righteousness to everyone who believes.[2]

### The Message of Salvation to All

[5] For Moses writes about the righteousness that is based on the law, that the person who does the commandments shall live by them. [6] But the righteousness based on faith says, "Do not say in your heart, 'Who will ascend into heaven?'" (that is, to bring Christ down) [7] "or 'Who will descend into the abyss?'" (that is, to bring Christ up from the dead). [8] But what does it say? [a] "The word is near you, in your mouth and in your heart" (that is, the word of faith that we proclaim); [9] because, if you confess with your mouth that Jesus is Lord and believe in your heart that God raised him from the dead, you will be saved. [10] For with the heart one believes and is justified, and with the mouth one confesses and is saved. [11] For the Scripture says, "Everyone who believes

---

[1] Or Brothers and sisters  [2] Or end of the law, that everyone who believes may be justified  [a] Deut. 30:14

..............................................................................................................

Christ will not experience **shame** on the day of judgment.

**10:2** The Jews' **zeal** and sincerity does not lead them to salvation. Many sincere "religious" people are wrong in their beliefs.

**10:3** On the contrast between the two ways to **righteousness**, see Gal. 3:7–14.

**10:4** **End** probably includes the idea of both goal and completion. The Mosaic law has reached its goal in Christ. Now the old covenant has ended. Since Christ is the goal and end of the law, **righteousness** belongs to all who trust in Christ.

**10:5** Paul quotes Lev. 18:5 regarding **the righteousness that is based on the law.** All those who keep the law will have life. But as Paul has already shown, all people violate the law (Rom. 1:18–3:20).

**10:6–8** Paul quotes Deut. 30:12–14 to show the contrast between the **righteousness based on faith** and the righteousness that comes from the law.

There is no need to travel to **heaven** to **bring Christ** to earth, for God has already sent him into the world. Nor should anyone think they must **bring Christ up from** the realm of **the dead,** for God has raised Christ from the dead. What God requires is not superhuman works but faith in the gospel.

**10:9–10** **if you confess with your mouth.** Such confession gives outward evidence of inward faith, and often confirms that faith to the speaker. **That God raised him from the dead** implies a belief in all truth connected with the resurrection. This includes Jesus' sin-bearing death, followed by his resurrection that showed God's approval of his work (see note on 4:25). **with the heart one believes.** Saving faith is deep trust in Christ.

**10:11** Paul again cites Isa. 28:16 (cf. Rom. 9:33) to emphasize that trusting in Christ (rather than good works) is the way to salvation. **Shame** here is the humiliation that those judged on the last day will experience when they are sent to hell.

in him will not be put to shame." [12] For there is no distinction between Jew and Greek; for the same Lord is Lord of all, bestowing his riches on all who call on him. [13] For [a] "everyone who calls on the name of the Lord will be saved."

[14] How then will they call on him in whom they have not believed? And how are they to believe in him of whom they have never heard?[1] And how are they to hear without someone preaching? [15] And how are they to preach unless they are sent? As it is written, [b] "How beautiful are the feet of those who preach the good news!" [16] But they have not all obeyed the gospel. For Isaiah says, [c] "Lord, who has believed what he has heard from us?" [17] So faith comes from hearing, and hearing through the word of Christ.

[18] But I ask, have they not heard? Indeed they have, for

[d] "Their voice has gone out to all the earth,

and their words to the ends of the world."

[19] But I ask, did Israel not understand? First Moses says,

[e] "I will make you jealous of those who are not a nation;

with a foolish nation I will make you angry."

[1] Or him whom they have never heard  [a] Joel 2:32  [b] Isa. 52:7  [c] Isa. 53:1  [d] Ps. 19:4  [e] Deut. 32:21

---

**10:14–15 How then?** With a series of rhetorical questions, Paul considers the chain of events necessary for a person to be saved. The logic of these verses is clear: (1) People will call on Jesus to save them only if they believe he can do so; (2) belief in Christ cannot exist without knowledge about him; (3) one hears about Christ only when someone proclaims the saving message; and (4) the message about Christ will not be proclaimed unless someone is sent by God to do so. Paul was so urgent about spreading the gospel to the ends of the earth because he believed that the only way to be saved was to hear and believe in the gospel. (Paul is not talking here about OT believers or infants). **beautiful . . . feet.** See Isa. 52:7.

**10:16 Isaiah** (Isa. 53:1) prophesies that not all will believe. In the context of Romans 9–11, Paul is thinking especially of unbelieving Jews.

**10:17** One can come to **faith** only through **hearing** the **word of Christ**, that is, the good news about Jesus Christ as the crucified and risen Savior.

**10:18–19** They who have heard the message probably refers to the Jewish people (see vv. 1, 19–20). Paul applies Ps. 19:4 to the proclamation of the gospel to emphasize that the Jews have heard the good news because the gospel has gone even **to the ends of the world** (that is, to the Gentiles). Israel should have understood from the prophecy of Deut. 32:21 that the Gentiles would believe.

²⁰ Then Isaiah is so bold as to say,

> ᵃ"I have been found by those who did not seek me;
>
> I have shown myself to those who did not ask for me."

²¹ But of Israel he says, ᵇ"All day long I have held out my hands to a disobedient and contrary people."

### The Remnant of Israel

11 I ask, then, has God rejected his people? By no means! For I myself am an Israelite, a descendant of Abraham,¹ a member of the tribe of Benjamin. ² God has not rejected his people whom he foreknew. Do you not know what the Scripture says of Elijah, how he appeals to God against Israel? ³ᶜ"Lord, they have killed your prophets, they have demolished your altars, and I alone am left, and they seek my life." ⁴ But what is God's reply to him? ᵈ"I have kept for myself seven thousand men who have not bowed the knee to Baal." ⁵ So too at the present time there is a remnant, chosen by grace. ⁶ But if it is by grace, it is no longer on the basis of works; otherwise grace would no longer be grace.

⁷ What then? Israel failed to obtain what it was seeking. The elect obtained it, but the rest were hardened, ⁸ as it is written,

¹ Or *one of the offspring of Abraham* ᵃ Isa. 65:1 ᵇ Isa. 65:2 ᶜ 1 Kgs. 19:10, 14 ᵈ 1 Kgs. 19:18

**10:20–21** Isaiah 65:1 has been fulfilled. Gentiles **who did not seek** after God have now experienced God's saving promises. Israel, on the other hand, has fulfilled the words of Isa. 65:2. They have rebelled and disobeyed the gospel message.

**11:1** The majority of Israel failed to believe. Does this mean that God has **rejected his people?** Paul presents himself as an example of the remnant that has been preserved. This remnant shows that God is not finished with Israel. He will fulfill his promises to his people.

**11:2 foreknew.** See note on 8:29.

**11:3–5** God assured Elijah that he had preserved a **remnant** who still followed him (1 Kings 19:18). As in Paul's day and today, a remnant of Jews believe in Christ because of God's electing grace (see Rom. 9:27–29).

**11:7–10** Paul links Isa. 29:10 and Deut. 29:4 to clarify that God has **hardened** Israel so that they would not see or hear. Paul then prays for judgment (Ps. 69:22–23) upon the Jews of his day who have rejected Christ.

> "God gave them a spirit of stupor,
>
> > eyes that would not see
> >
> > and ears that would not hear,
> >
> > down to this very day."

[9] And David says,

> [a] "Let their table become a snare and a trap,
>
> > a stumbling block and a retribution for them;
>
> [10]   let their eyes be darkened so that they cannot see,
>
> > and bend their backs forever."

## Gentiles Grafted In

[11] So I ask, did they stumble in order that they might fall? By no means! Rather, through their trespass salvation has come to the Gentiles, so as to make Israel jealous. [12] Now if their trespass means riches for the world, and if their failure means riches for the Gentiles, how much more will their full inclusion[1] mean!

[13] Now I am speaking to you Gentiles. Inasmuch then as I am an apostle to the Gentiles, I magnify my ministry [14] in order somehow to make my fellow Jews jealous, and thus save some of them. [15] For if their rejection means the reconciliation of the world, what will their acceptance mean

[1] Greek *their fullness*  [a] Ps. 69:22, 23

..................................................................................

**11:11–32** God's saving righteousness is seen in the salvation of Israel at the end of history, and in his saving plan for both Jews and Gentiles.

**11:12** World means **Gentiles** here. Paul argues from the lesser to the greater. If Israel's sin brought salvation to the Gentiles, then the blessing will be even greater when all Israel is saved (see v. 15).

**11:15** If the **rejection** of the majority of Israel has meant that many Gentiles (**the world**) have been reconciled to God through Christ, then surely the **acceptance** of the Jews—their future coming to Christ in large numbers—will bring about the final resurrection (**life from the dead**) and the end of history.

but life from the dead? [16] If the dough offered as firstfruits is holy, so is the whole lump, and if the root is holy, so are the branches.

[17] But if some of the branches were broken off, and you, although a wild olive shoot, were grafted in among the others and now share in the nourishing root[1] of the olive tree, [18] do not be arrogant toward the branches. If you are, remember it is not you who support the root, but the root that supports you. [19] Then you will say, "Branches were broken off so that I might be grafted in." [20] That is true. They were broken off because of their unbelief, but you stand fast through faith. So do not become proud, but fear. [21] For if God did not spare the natural branches, neither will he spare you. [22] Note then the kindness and the severity of God: severity toward those who have fallen, but God's kindness to you, provided you continue in his kindness. Otherwise you too will be cut off. [23] And even they, if they do not continue in their unbelief, will be grafted in, for God has the power to graft them in again. [24] For if you were cut from what is by nature a wild olive tree, and grafted, contrary to nature, into a cultivated olive tree, how much more will these, the natural branches, be grafted back into their own olive tree.

[1] Greek *root of richness*; some manuscripts *richness*

**11:16** Two illustrations teach the same truth. The **firstfruits** and the **root** probably refer to the patriarchs (Abraham, Isaac, and Jacob) and the saving promises given to them. If the firstfruits and root are dedicated to God, so too are the **whole lump** (of **dough**) and **the branches** (that is, the Jewish people as a whole). As Paul has already explained in chs. 9–10, however, not every Jewish person will be saved.

**11:17** The people of God are portrayed here as an **olive tree** (see Jer. 11:16–19; Hos. 14:6–7). When Paul says **some** branches were removed, he probably has in mind the majority of the Jews of his day. Gentiles are the **wild** shoots grafted into the olive tree that now share in the **root** (the promises made to the patriarchs).

**11:18–20** Gentile believers are warned against arrogance toward the Jews who were removed (v. 17). It is God's saving promises (**the root**), not their own goodness, that saved them. This should provoke **fear** and awe, not pride.

**11:21** Whether Jew or Gentile, God will not **spare** anyone who does not continue to believe.

**11:22–24** The Gentile readers must contemplate both God's **kindness** and his **severity** toward them and the Jews who have not believed. They must continue in faith. Otherwise, they too will be judged as unbelievers. Paul argues from the lesser to the greater. If God **grafted** Gentiles, who are the wild branches, into the olive tree, then surely he will graft back into the olive tree Jews, who are the **natural branches** (see v. 17).

*The Mystery of Israel's Salvation*

²⁵ Lest you be wise in your own sight, I do not want you to be unaware of this mystery, brothers:¹ a partial hardening has come upon Israel, until the fullness of the Gentiles has come in. ²⁶ And in this way all Israel will be saved, as it is written,

> ᵃ "The Deliverer will come from Zion,
>
>    he will banish ungodliness from Jacob";
>
> ²⁷   "and this will be my covenant with them
>
>    when I take away their sins."

²⁸ As regards the gospel, they are enemies for your sake. But as regards election, they are beloved for the sake of their forefathers. ²⁹ For the gifts and the calling of God are irrevocable. ³⁰ For just as you were at one time disobedient to God but now have received mercy because of their disobedience, ³¹ so they too have now been disobedient in order that by the mercy shown to you they also may now² receive mercy. ³² For God has consigned all to disobedience, that he may have mercy on all.

¹ Or *brothers and sisters*  ² Some manuscripts omit *now*  ᵃ Isa. 59:20, 21

**11:25 Mystery** in this case is something previously hidden that is now revealed.

**11:26 in this way all Israel will be saved.** It seems most likely that this salvation of the Jewish people is in the future. This interpretation fits with the promises of God's future work in vv. 12 and 15, and the future salvation of ethnic Israel at the end of history agrees with the character of this passage. God is faithful to fulfill his saving promises to his people (9:6). "All Israel" refers to a very large number, at least the majority of Jews. **The Deliverer** coming from Zion probably refers to Christ (see 1 Thess. 1:10), suggesting that these Jews will be saved near or at Christ's second coming.

**11:28 for your sake.** Israel's unbelief has benefited the Gentiles. This is the period of history in which Gentiles are being saved, while most of Israel remains in unbelief. But God's promise to **their forefathers** Abraham, Isaac, and Jacob will be fulfilled in the future.

**11:29** Israel will be saved because God always keeps his promises. As used here, **gifts** means the unique blessings given to Israel which Paul mentioned at the beginning of this long section (9:4–5). **Calling** refers here to calling to salvation (see 8:30; 9:11, 24).

**11:30–31** God saved the Gentiles when one would have expected only the Jews to be saved. In the future he will amaze all by saving the Jews. It will be clear that everyone's salvation is by **mercy** alone (see note on 9:14–16). The final **now** in the text means that the promise of Jewish salvation could be fulfilled at any time.

**11:32** The word **all** here refers to Jews and Gentiles. God's mercy is available to all, but not all will accept it.

[33] Oh, the depth of the riches and wisdom and knowledge of God! How unsearchable are his judgments and how inscrutable his ways!

[34]  "For who has known the mind of the Lord,

  or who has been his counselor?"

[35]  "Or who has given a gift to him

  that he might be repaid?"

[36] For from him and through him and to him are all things. To him be glory forever. Amen.

### A Living Sacrifice

12 I appeal to you therefore, brothers,[1] by the mercies of God, to present your bodies as a living sacrifice, holy and acceptable to God, which is your spiritual worship.[2] [2] Do not be conformed to this world,[3] but be transformed by the renewal of your mind, that by testing you may discern what is the will of God, what is good and acceptable and perfect.[4]

### Gifts of Grace

[3] For by the grace given to me I say to everyone among you not to think of himself more highly than he ought to think, but to think with sober

[1] Or brothers and sisters  [2] Or your rational service  [3] Greek age  [4] Or what is the good and acceptable and perfect will of God

**11:34–35** Paul quotes Isa. 40:13 and Job 41:11 to highlight that all good things are gifts from God (1 Cor. 4:7).

**12:1–15:13 God's Righteousness in Everyday Life.** The gift of God's saving righteousness leads to a new life. Paul explains some practical results of God's saving mercy.

**12:1 Therefore** points back to the entire argument in 1:18–11:36. **mercies of God.** Sacrificial language from the OT is used to describe the new life of Christians. **Bodies** refers to the whole person. Both body and soul belong to God. Christians are a **living sacrifice.** They enjoy new life with Christ (6:4). "Living" also means that they will not be put to death as OT animal sacrifices were. **Spiritual worship** means offering one's whole life to God (see Heb. 13:15–16).

**12:2** The present evil age still tempts Christians, so they must resist its pressure. Their minds are made new (contrast 1:28), so that they are able to "discern" or understand God's will. **By testing you may discern** translates a Greek word that means finding out the worth of something by testing it.

judgment, each according to the measure of faith that God has assigned. [4] For as in one body we have many members,[1] and the members do not all have the same function, [5] so we, though many, are one body in Christ, and individually members one of another. [6] Having gifts that differ according to the grace given to us, let us use them: if prophecy, in proportion to our faith; [7] if service, in our serving; the one who teaches, in his teaching; [8] the one who exhorts, in his exhortation; the one who contributes, in generosity; the one who leads,[2] with zeal; the one who does acts of mercy, with cheerfulness.

## Marks of the True Christian

[9] Let love be genuine. Abhor what is evil; hold fast to what is good. [10] Love one another with brotherly affection. Outdo one another in showing honor. [11] Do not be slothful in zeal, be fervent in spirit,[3] serve the Lord. [12] Rejoice in hope, be patient in tribulation, be constant in prayer. [13] Contribute to the needs of the saints and seek to show hospitality.

[14] Bless those who persecute you; bless and do not curse them. [15] Rejoice with those who rejoice, weep with those who weep. [16] Live in harmony with one another. Do not be haughty, but associate with the lowly.[4] Never be wise in your own sight. [17] Repay no one evil for evil, but give thought to

[1] Greek *parts*; also verse 5  [2] Or *gives aid*  [3] Or *fervent in the Spirit*  [4] Or *give yourselves to humble tasks*

**12:4–5** The diversity and unity of the church is compared to the human body. (See also 1 Corinthians 12 and Eph. 4:4, 12–16.)

For an additional resource on Paul's teachings on spiritual gifts, see p. 115.

**12:6 Prophecy.** Generally refers to something God reveals to an individual in a particular situation, which must be evaluated by other believers (see 1 Cor. 12:10; 1 Thess. 5:20–21). True prophecy agrees with Scripture and helps the church. **in proportion to our faith.** Those with the gift of prophecy should speak only when they are confident that the Holy Spirit is truly revealing something to them.

**12:7–8** Christians should use the gifts God has given them, whether in **serving** others, **teaching** God's Word, or in **exhortation** and encouragement.

**12:9** The rest of the chapter describes the life that pleases God. Not surprisingly, **love** heads the list.

**12:13 Hospitality** was very important for early Christians, because most of them could not afford to pay for lodging when traveling.

**12:14 Bless . . . do not curse.** These words reflect the teaching of Jesus (Matt. 5:44).

**12:17–19 Repay no one evil. . . . Vengeance is mine.** This alludes to Jesus' teaching (Matt. 5:39).

do what is honorable in the sight of all. **¹⁸** If possible, so far as it depends on you, live peaceably with all. **¹⁹** Beloved, never avenge yourselves, but leave it¹ to the wrath of God, for it is written, ᵃ "Vengeance is mine, I will repay, says the Lord." **²⁰** To the contrary, ᵇ "if your enemy is hungry, feed him; if he is thirsty, give him something to drink; for by so doing you will heap burning coals on his head." **²¹** Do not be overcome by evil, but overcome evil with good.

### Submission to the Authorities

**13** Let every person be subject to the governing authorities. For there is no authority except from God, and those that exist have been instituted by God. **²** Therefore whoever resists the authorities resists what God has appointed, and those who resist will incur judgment. **³** For rulers are not a terror to good conduct, but to bad. Would you have no fear of the one who is in authority? Then do what is good, and you will receive his approval, **⁴** for he is God's servant for your good. But if you do wrong, be afraid, for he does not bear the sword in vain. For he is the servant of God, an avenger

¹ Greek *give place*  ᵃ Deut. 32:35  ᵇ Prov. 25:21, 22

...........................................................................................................

**12:20-21 burning coals.** See Prov. 25:21-22. Most interpreters think Paul is teaching that Christians must do good to people so that the others will feel ashamed and repent. That sense is possible. But in the OT the concept of "burning coals" always represents punishment (see Ps. 11:6). Thus another interpretation is that Paul is repeating the thought of Rom. 12:19: Christians are to do good to wrong-doers, whom God will punish on the last day if they refuse to repent. Overcoming **evil with good** includes acts of kindness toward evildoers. It may sometimes include the "good" (13:4) of the civil government stopping evil through the use of force (military or police). See 13:3-4.

**13:1-7** Christians are to **be subject to** (which generally means to obey, see 1 Pet. 3:5-6) the government because it has been put in place by God. Several other passages show that God approves of Christians disobeying government, but only when

obedience to government would mean disobeying God (see Ex. 1:17, 21; Est. 4:16; Dan. 3:12-18; Acts 5:29; Heb. 11:23).

**13:1** Sometimes God gives good authorities as a blessing, and sometimes he allows evil rulers as a means of trial or judgment (2 Chron. 25:20; 32:24-25). On God's rule over earthly **authorities**, see Ps. 75:7 and Dan. 2:21.

**13:3 rulers are not a terror to good conduct, but to bad.** Civil government in general is a great blessing from God.

**13:4** Governing authorities are God's servants, for they carry out his **wrath** on evildoers, and they do so **for your good.** Even though Christians must not take personal revenge (12:17-20), it is right for them to turn punishment over to the civil authorities, who have the responsibility to punish evil. **Sword** most likely refers to capital punishment (see Gen. 9:6).

who carries out God's wrath on the wrongdoer. [5] Therefore one must be in subjection, not only to avoid God's wrath but also for the sake of conscience. [6] For because of this you also pay taxes, for the authorities are ministers of God, attending to this very thing. [7] Pay to all what is owed to them: taxes to whom taxes are owed, revenue to whom revenue is owed, respect to whom respect is owed, honor to whom honor is owed.

### Fulfilling the Law Through Love

[8] Owe no one anything, except to love each other, for the one who loves another has fulfilled the law. [9] For the commandments, [a] "You shall not commit adultery, You shall not murder, You shall not steal, You shall not covet," and any other commandment, are summed up in this word: [b] "You shall love your neighbor as yourself." [10] Love does no wrong to a neighbor; therefore love is the fulfilling of the law.

[11] Besides this you know the time, that the hour has come for you to wake from sleep. For salvation is nearer to us now than when we first believed. [12] The night is far gone; the day is at hand. So then let us cast off the works of darkness and put on the armor of light. [13] Let us walk properly as in the daytime, not in orgies and drunkenness, not in sexual immorality and sensuality, not in quarreling and jealousy. [14] But put on the Lord Jesus Christ, and make no provision for the flesh, to gratify its desires.

[a] Ex. 20:13-17; Deut. 5:17-21  [b] Lev. 19:18

**13:5** Christians should obey civil authorities to avoid God's wrath (coming through those authorities, v. 4) and because their conscience tells them to submit to the government (see note on vv. 1-7).

**13:8** Verses 8-10 focus on the Christian's relationship to the Mosaic law. Owe no one anything does not prohibit all borrowing. It means that one should always "pay what is owed" (see v. 7), fulfilling whatever agreements have been made.

**13:9** Paul cites several OT commandments regarding responsibility to others. All of these are summarized in the call to love your neighbor as yourself (Lev. 19:18).

**13:11-12** The final verses of this section (12:3-13:14) call Christians to action, given the shortness of the time before Jesus returns.

**13:14** The metaphor of putting on clothing implies imitating Christ's character and living in close fellowship with him. This requires denying the flesh and refusing to gratify its desires.

*Do Not Pass Judgment on One Another*

**14** As for the one who is weak in faith, welcome him, but not to quarrel over opinions. [2] One person believes he may eat anything, while the weak person eats only vegetables. [3] Let not the one who eats despise the one who abstains, and let not the one who abstains pass judgment on the one who eats, for God has welcomed him. [4] Who are you to pass judgment on the servant of another? It is before his own master[1] that he stands or falls. And he will be upheld, for the Lord is able to make him stand.

[5] One person esteems one day as better than another, while another esteems all days alike. Each one should be fully convinced in his own mind. [6] The one who observes the day, observes it in honor of the Lord. The one who eats, eats in honor of the Lord, since he gives thanks to God, while the one who abstains, abstains in honor of the Lord and gives thanks to God. [7] For none of us lives to himself, and none of us dies to himself. [8] For if we live, we live to the Lord, and if we die, we die to the Lord. So then, whether we live or whether we die, we are the Lord's. [9] For to this end Christ died and lived again, that he might be Lord both of the dead and of the living.

[1] Or *lord*

14:1–15:13 Paul addresses a specific dispute, probably over whether Christians need to follow Jewish food laws. He agrees with the "strong" (who did not feel compelled to follow those laws), but he encourages them not to despise or offend the "weak."

14:1 **As for the one who is weak.** The strong are tempted to argue with those weaker in faith.

14:2 The strong believe all foods are allowed. The weak eat only **vegetables**, probably to avoid eating unclean foods (see Dan. 1:8, 10, 12, 16).

14:4 This verse is likely directed to the weak. They are not to **pass judgment** on the strong, who answer to their **own master** (**the Lord**).

14:5 The weak thought some days were more important than others. Given the Jewish background (see v. 14), the **day** is the Sabbath. The strong think every day is the same. Both views are fine. Each person must follow his own conscience. Unlike the other nine commandments in Ex. 20:1–17, the Sabbath commandment seems to have been part of the "ceremonial laws" of the Mosaic covenant. Like the laws about sacrifices and diet, sabbath observance is not binding on new covenant believers (see also Gal. 4:10; Col. 2:16–17). However, regular times of worship are commanded for Christians (Heb. 10:24–25; see Acts 20:7).

[10] Why do you pass judgment on your brother? Or you, why do you despise your brother? For we will all stand before the judgment seat of God; [11] for it is written,

> [a] "As I live, says the Lord, every knee shall bow to me,
>
> and every tongue shall confess[1] to God."

[12] So then each of us will give an account of himself to God.

## Do Not Cause Another to Stumble

[13] Therefore let us not pass judgment on one another any longer, but rather decide never to put a stumbling block or hindrance in the way of a brother. [14] I know and am persuaded in the Lord Jesus that nothing is unclean in itself, but it is unclean for anyone who thinks it unclean. [15] For if your brother is grieved by what you eat, you are no longer walking in love. By what you eat, do not destroy the one for whom Christ died. [16] So do not let what you regard as good be spoken of as evil. [17] For the kingdom of God is not a matter of eating and drinking but of righteousness and peace and joy in the Holy Spirit. [18] Whoever thus serves Christ is acceptable to God and approved by men. [19] So then let us pursue what makes for peace and for mutual upbuilding.

[1] Or *shall give praise* [a] Isa. 45:23

**14:10-12** The strong should not despise the weak. The weak should not judge the strong. Everyone will stand before God, who will judge all on the last day. The future day of **judgment** is prophesied in Isa. 45:23. Every person will give **an account** of his life to God at the judgment.

**14:14** Christians are no longer under the old covenant, so Paul rejects the view that some foods are **unclean** (see Leviticus 11; Deuteronomy 14). Still, if anyone thinks certain foods are unclean, then that person should avoid them.

**14:15-17** For the sake of the weak, the strong should refrain from eating certain foods. They must be careful not to **destroy** the faith of a brother or sister. Lack of love for the weak contradicts Christ's love. God's kingdom centers on the gifts of **righteousness**, **peace**, and **joy** granted by the Holy Spirit. Bodily appetites are secondary in importance.

[20] Do not, for the sake of food, destroy the work of God. Everything is indeed clean, but it is wrong for anyone to make another stumble by what he eats. [21] It is good not to eat meat or drink wine or do anything that causes your brother to stumble.[1] [22] The faith that you have, keep between yourself and God. Blessed is the one who has no reason to pass judgment on himself for what he approves. [23] But whoever has doubts is condemned if he eats, because the eating is not from faith. For whatever does not proceed from faith is sin.[2]

### The Example of Christ

15 We who are strong have an obligation to bear with the failings of the weak, and not to please ourselves. [2] Let each of us please his neighbor for his good, to build him up. [3] For Christ did not please himself, but as it is written, [a] "The reproaches of those who reproached you fell on me." [4] For whatever was written in former days was written for our instruction, that through endurance and through the encouragement of the Scriptures we might have hope. [5] May the God of endurance and encouragement grant you to live in such harmony with one another, in accord with Christ Jesus, [6] that together you may with one voice glorify the God and Father of our Lord Jesus Christ. [7] Therefore welcome one another as Christ has welcomed you, for the glory of God.

[1] Some manuscripts add *or be hindered or be weakened* [2] Some manuscripts insert here 16:25–27 [a] Ps. 69:9

**14:20–21** Paul urges the strong not to **destroy** God's **work** in the weak by eating **food** that will offend them.

**14:22** The strong are likely addressed here. **The faith that you have** means their faith that they may eat anything (see vv. 1–2, 23). They are not asked to change their convictions, but they should not behave in a way that injures the faith of others and so brings **judgment** on themselves.

**14:23** No one should eat unclean food if he has **doubts** about the rightness of the activity. Indeed, anything believers do apart from **faith** is sin.

**15:1–3** Christ is the supreme example of strengthening others and living for the glory of God. Paul quotes Ps. 69:9 to make this point.

**15:4 for our instruction . . . encouragement.** All the words of the OT are the words of God. They teach believers how to live in a way that pleases God.

*Christ the Hope of Jews and Gentiles*

⁸ For I tell you that Christ became a servant to the circumcised to show God's truthfulness, in order to confirm the promises given to the patriarchs, ⁹ and in order that the Gentiles might glorify God for his mercy. As it is written,

> ᵃ "Therefore I will praise you among the Gentiles,
>
>     and sing to your name."

¹⁰ And again it is said,

> ᵇ "Rejoice, O Gentiles, with his people."

¹¹ And again,

> ᶜ "Praise the Lord, all you Gentiles,
>
>     and let all the peoples extol him."

¹² And again Isaiah says,

> ᵈ "The root of Jesse will come,
>
>     even he who arises to rule the Gentiles;
>
>     in him will the Gentiles hope."

¹³ May the God of hope fill you with all joy and peace in believing, so that by the power of the Holy Spirit you may abound in hope.

ᵃ 2 Sam. 22:50; Ps. 18:49 ᵇ Deut. 32:43 ᶜ Ps. 117:1 ᵈ Isa. 11:10

**15:8 circumcised**. The Jews. In fulfilling God's saving promises to the Jews, God shows **truthfulness** and faithfulness to his word.

**15:9–12** Paul cites verses from 2 Sam. 22:50 (or Ps. 18:49); Deut. 32:43; Ps. 117:1; and Isa. 11:10. The OT clearly emphasizes the inclusion of the **Gentiles** into the people of God.

*Paul the Minister to the Gentiles*

[14] I myself am satisfied about you, my brothers,[1] that you yourselves are full of goodness, filled with all knowledge and able to instruct one another. [15] But on some points I have written to you very boldly by way of reminder, because of the grace given me by God [16] to be a minister of Christ Jesus to the Gentiles in the priestly service of the gospel of God, so that the offering of the Gentiles may be acceptable, sanctified by the Holy Spirit. [17] In Christ Jesus, then, I have reason to be proud of my work for God. [18] For I will not venture to speak of anything except what Christ has accomplished through me to bring the Gentiles to obedience—by word and deed, [19] by the power of signs and wonders, by the power of the Spirit of God—so that from Jerusalem and all the way around to Illyricum I have fulfilled the ministry of the gospel of Christ; [20] and thus I make it my ambition to preach the gospel, not where Christ has already been named, lest I build on someone else's foundation, [21] but as it is written,

[a] "Those who have never been told of him will see,

and those who have never heard will understand."

[1] Or *brothers and sisters;* also verse 30  [a] Isa. 52:15

---

**15:14–16:23 The Extension of God's Righteousness through Paul's Mission.** Paul focuses on his calling as the apostle to the Gentiles, adding some greetings and final instructions.

**15:14 Instruct** often means warning against wrong conduct (cf. 1 Cor. 4:14; 1 Thess. 5:12, 14; 2 Thess. 3:15).

**15:16** Gentile converts are **the offering** Paul presents to God.

**15:19 By the power of signs and wonders** refers to the miracles God did through Paul during his min-istry. Miracles pointed to the power of God (see Acts 5:12; 2 Cor. 12:12; Heb. 2:4). Paul has fulfilled his charge to preach the gospel among the Gentiles from **Jerusalem** to **Illyricum** (roughly the area that is now Albania and was formerly Yugoslavia). Churches have been planted in key places. From there Paul's coworkers will bring the gospel to more remote areas (e.g., Epaphras in Colossae, Col. 1:7).

**15:20–21** Paul's aim was **to preach the gospel** where no churches existed, fulfilling Isa. 52:15.

*Paul's Plan to Visit Rome*

²²This is the reason why I have so often been hindered from coming to you. ²³But now, since I no longer have any room for work in these regions, and since I have longed for many years to come to you, ²⁴I hope to see you in passing as I go to Spain, and to be helped on my journey there by you, once I have enjoyed your company for a while. ²⁵At present, however, I am going to Jerusalem bringing aid to the saints. ²⁶For Macedonia and Achaia have been pleased to make some contribution for the poor among the saints at Jerusalem. ²⁷For they were pleased to do it, and indeed they owe it to them. For if the Gentiles have come to share in their spiritual blessings, they ought also to be of service to them in material blessings. ²⁸When therefore I have completed this and have delivered to them what has been collected,[1] I will leave for Spain by way of you. ²⁹I know that when I come to you I will come in the fullness of the blessing[2] of Christ.

³⁰I appeal to you, brothers, by our Lord Jesus Christ and by the love of the Spirit, to strive together with me in your prayers to God on my behalf, ³¹that I may be delivered from the unbelievers in Judea, and that my service for Jerusalem may be acceptable to the saints, ³²so that by God's will I may come to you with joy and be refreshed in your company. ³³May the God of peace be with you all. Amen.

[1] Greek *sealed to them this fruit*  [2] Some manuscripts insert *of the gospel*

---

**15:22-24** Paul had been stopped from coming to Rome because he had not completed his work of planting churches in unreached eastern parts of the Roman Empire (v. 22), but now he feels that his work in the east has come to an end (vv. 23-24). He hopes to see the Roman church. He wants them to be his base of support for his mission to **Spain**. No visit of Paul to Spain is recorded in the NT. It is possible that he went there after the events recorded in Acts 28:30-31.

**15:25** He cannot visit Rome immediately. Paul's next task is to travel to **Jerusalem** to bring the money he had collected for the poor saints there (see 1 Cor. 16:1-4; 2 Corinthians 8-9).

**15:26 Macedonia and Achaia** are roughly equivalent to northern and southern Greece today, including such cities as Philippi, Thessalonica, and Corinth.

**15:27 they were pleased.** The Gentiles enjoy the **spiritual blessings** of the Jewish people. They should happily assist them financially.

**15:31 delivered from the unbelievers.** Paul did go to Rome, even if it was not in the way he anticipated (see Acts 22-28).

*Personal Greetings*

**16** I commend to you our sister Phoebe, a servant[1] of the church at Cenchreae, [2] that you may welcome her in the Lord in a way worthy of the saints, and help her in whatever she may need from you, for she has been a patron of many and of myself as well.

[3] Greet Prisca and Aquila, my fellow workers in Christ Jesus, [4] who risked their necks for my life, to whom not only I give thanks but all the churches of the Gentiles give thanks as well. [5] Greet also the church in their house. Greet my beloved Epaenetus, who was the first convert[2] to Christ in Asia. [6] Greet Mary, who has worked hard for you. [7] Greet Andronicus and Junia,[3] my kinsmen and my fellow prisoners. They are well known to the apostles,[4] and they were in Christ before me. [8] Greet Ampliatus, my beloved in the Lord. [9] Greet Urbanus, our fellow worker in Christ, and my beloved Stachys. [10] Greet Apelles, who is approved in Christ. Greet those who belong to the family of Aristobulus. [11] Greet my kinsman Herodion.

[1] Or *deaconess* [2] Greek *firstfruit* [3] Or *Junias* [4] Or *messengers*

---

**16:1-23** Paul warmly greets those he knows in Rome. He is able to say something specific about almost every person greeted.

**16:1 Phoebe** probably brought this epistle to the Romans. **servant.** The Greek word can mean either "servant" (13:4; 15:8; 1 Cor. 3:5; 1 Tim. 4:6) or "deacon" (referring to a church office; Phil. 1:1; 1 Tim. 3:8, 12).

**16:2** Paul asks the church to assist Phoebe since she has helped so many. Phoebe served as a **patron**, probably offering financial assistance and hospitality to other believers.

**16:3 Prisca and Aquila.** See 1 Cor. 16:19; 2 Tim. 4:19. Prisca is called Priscilla in Acts 18:2-3, 18, 26.

**16:4** Perhaps Prisca and Aquila **risked** their lives when Paul was in danger in Ephesus (Acts 19:23-41; 1 Cor. 15:32; 2 Cor. 1:8-11).

**16:5 the church in their house.** Apparently a church met in the home of Prisca and Aquila. **Asia** here refers to a province in what is modern-day Turkey.

**16:7 Andronicus and Junia** were probably a hus-band-and-wife ministry team. Most scholars now think that Junia was a woman, though some have argued that a man named Junias is in view (the spelling would be the same in Greek). The verse seems to be saying that Andronicus and Junia were **well known to the apostles**, not that Junia was herself an apostle. This passage also reveals that the couple was Jewish, had been imprisoned, and had become Christians before Paul.

**16:8-10** The people greeted in these verses are not mentioned elsewhere in the NT. The **family of Aristobulus** probably refers to the slaves in Aristobulus's household. Some think Aristobulus is the grandson of Herod the Great (c. 73-4 BC) and the brother of Herod Agrippa I (10 BC-AD 44).

**16:11** The **family of Narcissus** refers to the slaves in Narcissus's household. Some scholars think Narcissus was the wealthy freedman who served the emperor Claudius (AD 41-54). Nero's mother, Agrippina, forced Narcissus to kill himself when Nero became emperor (AD 54).

Greet those in the Lord who belong to the family of Narcissus. [12] Greet those workers in the Lord, Tryphaena and Tryphosa. Greet the beloved Persis, who has worked hard in the Lord. [13] Greet Rufus, chosen in the Lord; also his mother, who has been a mother to me as well. [14] Greet Asyncritus, Phlegon, Hermes, Patrobas, Hermas, and the brothers[1] who are with them. [15] Greet Philologus, Julia, Nereus and his sister, and Olympas, and all the saints who are with them. [16] Greet one another with a holy kiss. All the churches of Christ greet you.

## Final Instructions and Greetings

[17] I appeal to you, brothers, to watch out for those who cause divisions and create obstacles contrary to the doctrine that you have been taught; avoid them. [18] For such persons do not serve our Lord Christ, but their own appetites,[2] and by smooth talk and flattery they deceive the hearts of the naive. [19] For your obedience is known to all, so that I rejoice over you, but I want you to be wise as to what is good and innocent as to what is evil. [20] The God of peace will soon crush Satan under your feet. The grace of our Lord Jesus Christ be with you.

[21] Timothy, my fellow worker, greets you; so do Lucius and Jason and Sosipater, my kinsmen.

[22] I Tertius, who wrote this letter, greet you in the Lord.

[1] Or brothers and sisters; also verse 17  [2] Greek their own belly

**16:13** Rufus. Possibly the son of Simon of Cyrene (Mark 15:21). Apparently Rufus's mother ministered significantly to Paul.

**16:16** Christians greeted one another with a holy kiss to show their warm affection (also 1 Cor. 16:20; 2 Cor. 13:12; 1 Thess. 5:26; 1 Pet. 5:14).

**16:20** This is an allusion to Gen. 3:15.

**16:21** Those who are with Paul greet the Romans.

Timothy is probably Paul's most beloved coworker in ministry. Lucius is unknown. Jason is likely the same person named in Acts 17:5–7, 9. Sosipater is probably the same person as Sopater from Berea (Acts 20:4).

**16:22** Tertius functioned as Paul's secretary for the letter. It was common for those writing letters in the first century to dictate to a secretary, but the content of the letter is clearly Paul's.

[23] Gaius, who is host to me and to the whole church, greets you. Erastus,

the city treasurer, and our brother Quartus, greet you.[1]

## Doxology

[25] Now to him who is able to strengthen you according to my gospel and

the preaching of Jesus Christ, according to the revelation of the mystery that

was kept secret for long ages [26] but has now been disclosed and through the

prophetic writings has been made known to all nations, according to the

command of the eternal God, to bring about the obedience of faith— [27] to

the only wise God be glory forevermore through Jesus Christ! Amen.

[1] Some manuscripts insert verse 24: *The grace of our Lord Jesus Christ be with you all. Amen*

**16:23** Gaius here is the Gaius of 1 Cor. 1:14. This supports the idea that the letter was written from Corinth. He was a man of some wealth, for he provided a place for the entire church to meet. It is difficult to know if **Erastus** is the person mentioned in Acts 19:22 and 2 Tim. 4:20.

**16:25–27 Final Summary of the Gospel of God's Righteousness.** Many of the themes in the introduction reappear in the conclusion.

**16:26** prophetic writings. The OT Scriptures (see 1:2).

**16:27** glory forevermore. God's glory is to be the theme of Christians' lives and the joy of their hearts.

| OT Testimony That All Are under Sin (3:9) | |
| --- | --- |
| **Romans 3** | **OT Reference** |
| *Sinful Condition* | |
| v. 10, none is righteous | Ps. 14:3/53:3; Eccles. 7:20 |
| v. 11a, no one understands | Ps. 14:2/53:2 |
| v. 11b, no one seeks for God | Ps. 14:2/53:2 |
| v. 12, all have turned aside; together they have become worthless; no one does good, not even one | Ps. 14:3/53:3 |
| *Sinful Speech (note progression from throat to tongue to lips)* | |
| v. 13a, b, their throat is an open grave; they use their tongues to deceive | Ps. 5:9 (5:10, Septuagint) |
| v. 13c, the venom of asps is under their lips | Ps. 140:3 |
| v. 14, their mouth is full of curses and bitterness | Ps. 10:7 |
| *Sinful Action* | |
| v. 15, their feet are swift to shed blood | Prov. 1:16/Isa. 59:7 |
| v. 16, in their paths are ruin and misery | Isa. 59:7 |
| v. 17, and the way of peace they have not known | Isa. 59:8 |
| *Summary Statement* | |
| v. 18, there is no fear of God before their eyes | Ps. 36:1 |

## Spiritual Gifts in Paul's Letters

| Romans 12:6–8 | 1 Corinthians 12:7–10 | 1 Corinthians 12:28 | Ephesians 4:11 |
|---|---|---|---|
| *Having gifts that differ according to the grace given to us* | *To each is given the manifestation of the Spirit for the common good* | *God has appointed in the church* | *And he gave* |
| | | apostles | the apostles |
| prophecy | prophecy | prophets | the prophets |
| | | | the evangelists |
| | ability to distinguish between spirits | | |
| | utterance of wisdom | | |
| teaching | utterance of knowledge | teachers | the shepherds and teachers |
| exhorting | | | |
| | working of miracles | miracles | |
| | gifts of healing | gifts of healing | |
| service | | helping | |
| leading | | administrating | |
| | various kinds of tongues | various kinds of tongues | |
| | interpretation of tongues | | |
| giving | | | |
| | faith | | |
| mercy | | | |

# GLOSSARY

**Amen**
Greek form of a Hebrew word meaning "to confirm." In Scripture and in Christian life, when uttered after a prayer or statement, it means "let it be so."

**Antinomianism**
The false belief that OT moral laws are no longer necessary or binding for those living under grace (see Rom. 6:1–2).

**Atonement**
The reconciliation of a person with God, often associated with the offering of a sacrifice. Through his death and resurrection, Jesus Christ made atonement for the sins of believers (Rom. 3:25). His death satisfied God's just wrath against sinful humanity, just as OT sacrifices symbolized substitutionary death as payment for sin.

**Circumcision**
The ritual practice of removing the foreskin of an individual, which was commanded for all male Israelites in OT times as a sign of participation in the covenant God established with Abraham (Gen. 17:9–14).

**Conscience**
The ability to understand tacitly the rightness or wrongness of one's actions and motives. The conscience is not identical with the inner witness of the Holy Spirit, although the Holy Spirit often employs the conscience in guiding people and convicting them of sin (Rom. 2:15).

**Covenant**
A binding agreement between two parties, typically involving a formal statement of their relationship. This agreement includes a list of stipulations and obligations for both parties, a list of witnesses to the agreement, and a list of curses for unfaithfulness and blessings for faithfulness to the agreement. The OT is more properly understood as the old covenant, meaning the agreement established between God and his people prior to the coming of Jesus Christ to establish the new covenant (NT).

**Doxology**
Expression of praise to God. Often included at the end of NT letters (e.g., Rom. 16:25–27). Modern church services often end with doxologies in the form of short hymns.

**End Times**
A time associated with events prophesied in Scripture to occur at the end of the world and the second coming of Christ—also known as "the last days." The NT teaches that in Christ, the last days have dawned. The "end times" can refer, then, to the entire period in between Christ's first and second comings.

**Eschatology**
Study of the end times as described in the Bible. Includes such topics as the return of Christ, the period of tribulation, the resurrection and judgment of all people, and the millennial reign of Christ on earth.

**Glorification**
The work of God in believers to bring them to the ultimate and perfect stage of salvation—full Christlikeness—following his justification and sanctification of them (Rom. 8:29–30). Glorification includes believers receiving imperishable resurrection bodies at Christ's return (1 Cor. 15:42–43).

**Gospel**
A common translation for a Greek word meaning "good news," that is, the good news of Jesus Christ and the salvation he made possible by his crucifixion, burial, and resurrection. Gospel with an initial capital letter refers to each of the biblical accounts of Jesus' life on earth (Matthew, Mark, Luke, and John).

**Grace**
Unmerited favor, especially the free gift of salvation that God gives to believers through faith in Jesus Christ.

**Impute**
To attribute something to someone or credit it to his or her account. Often refers to God's crediting to every believer the righteousness of Jesus Christ (Rom. 4:22–25).

**Indwelling**
In Scripture, the word refers to the presence of Christ and the Holy Spirit within believers (Rom. 8:9–11; Eph. 3:16–19). This presence enables Christians to love (1 John 4:8–12) and to overcome sin, which also indwells believers but no longer defines them (Rom. 8:4–11).

### Intercede

To appeal to one person on behalf of another. Often used with reference to prayer.

### Justification

The act of God's grace in declaring sinners fully acquitted and counting them as righteous before him on the basis of the finished work of Christ, received through faith alone.

### Kingdom of God

The rule of God manifested in the long-awaited restoration of his people and indeed the whole world. When Jesus came two thousand years ago, he announced that the kingdom of God had arrived (Mark 1:15; Luke 17:20–21). Yet because of ongoing rebellion and rejection of Jesus and his rule, the kingdom still awaits its final consummation and fulfillment in Jesus' second coming (Mark 14:25). For this reason we pray for the kingdom to come (Matt. 6:10).

### Legalism

Requirements that go beyond the commands of Scripture; or the unbiblical belief that works are the means of becoming right with God (cf. Rom 3:19–20).

### Omniscience

An attribute of God that describes his complete knowledge and understanding of all things at all times (cf. Rom. 8:29).

### Predestination

God's sovereign choice of people for redemption and eternal life. Also referred to as "election."

### Propitiation

The appeasement of wrath by the offering of a gift or sacrifice. Jesus made propitiation for the sins of humanity by his suffering and death (Rom. 3:25; Heb. 2:17; 1 John 2:2; 4:10).

### Reconciliation

The restoration of an affirmative relationship and peace between alienated or opposing parties. Through his death and resurrection, Jesus has reconciled believers to God (2 Cor. 5:18–21).

### Remnant

In the Bible, a portion of people who remain after most others are destroyed by some catastrophe. The notion of a "remnant" can be found in various events recorded in Scripture, including the flood (Genesis 6–8) and the return of exiled Judah (Ezra 9).

### Repentance

A complete change of heart and mind regarding one's overall attitude toward God and one's individual actions. True regeneration and conversion is always accompanied by repentance.

### Righteousness

The quality of being morally right and without sin; one of God's distinctive attributes. God imputes righteousness to (i.e., justifies) those who trust in Jesus Christ.

### Sacrifice

An offering to God, often to signify forgiveness of sin. The law of Moses gave detailed instructions regarding various kinds of sacrifices. By his death on the cross, Jesus gave himself as a sacrifice to atone for the sins of believers (Eph. 5:2; Heb. 10:12). Believers are to offer their bodies as living sacrifices to God (Rom. 12:1).

### Sanctification

The process of being conformed to the image of Jesus Christ through the work of the Holy Spirit. This process begins immediately after regeneration and continues throughout a Christian's life, finally resulting in glorification.

### Satan

A spiritual being whose name means "accuser." As the leader of all the demonic forces, he opposes God's rule and seeks to harm God's people and accuse them of wrongdoing. His power, however, is confined to the bounds that God has set for him, and one day he will be destroyed along with all his demons (Matt. 25:41; Rev. 20:10).

### Sovereignty

Supreme and independent power and authority. Sovereignty over all things is a distinctive attribute of God (1 Tim. 6:15–16). He directs all things to carry out his purposes (Rom. 8:28–29).

### Substitutionary Atonement

The core reason for Jesus' death on the cross: identifying with his Father's will, Jesus offered himself to die as a substitute for believers. He took upon himself the punishment they deserve and thereby reconciled them to God (Romans 3).

### Transgression

A violation of a command or law.

### Typology

A method of biblical interpretation in which a real historical object, place, or person is recognized as a pattern or foreshadowing (a "type") of some later object, place, or person. For example, the Bible presents Adam as a "type" of Christ (Rom. 5:14).

### Universalism

The unbiblical belief that all people will be saved from eternal damnation, regardless of whether or not they come to faith in Christ. Romans 5:18 is sometimes used to support this idea, but in context it is clear Paul means not that all people but that people of all kinds will be saved.

# CONCORDANCE

## ABRAHAM
What then shall we say was gained by **A**,................4:1
For if **A** was justified by works,................4:2
"**A** believed God, and it was counted to him................4:3
that faith was counted to **A** as righteousness.................4:9
footsteps of the faith that our father **A** had................4:12
For the promise to **A** and his offspring that................4:13
but also to the one who shares the faith of **A**,...........4:16
and not all are children of **A** because they are.............9:7
Israelite, a descendant of **A**,................11:1

## ACCEPTABLE
bodies as a **a** living sacrifice, holy and **a** to God, ............12:1
will of God, what is good and **a** and perfect................12:2
Whoever thus serves Christ is **a** to God and ............14:18
that the offering of the Gentiles may be **a**, ................15:16
for Jerusalem may be **a** to the saints,...........15:31

## ADOPTION
you have received the Spirit of **a** as sons,................8:15
inwardly as we wait eagerly for **a** as sons, ................8:23
They are Israelites, and to them belong the **a**, ............9:4

## ALIVE
must consider yourselves dead to sin and **a** to God....6:11
she lives with another man while her husband is **a**.......7:3
I was once **a** apart from the law, but when the............7:9
commandment came, sin came **a** and I died................7:9

## BEAR
although the Law and the Prophets **b** witness to........3:21
in order that we may **b** fruit for God...................7:4
at work in our members to **b** fruit for death.................7:5
I **b** them witness that they have a zeal for God,............10:2
be afraid, for he does not **b** the sword in vain.............13:4
an obligation to **b** with the failings of the weak, ..........15:1

## BELIEVE
through faith in Jesus Christ for all who **b**................3:22
was to make him the father of all who **b**, ...............4:11
It will be counted to us who **b** in him who ................4:24
Christ, we **b** that we will also live with him. ................6:8
and **b** in your heart that God raised him from............10:9
And how are they to **b** in him of whom they .............10:14

## BELONG
including you who are called to **b** to Jesus Christ,........1:6
so that you may **b** to another, to him who has................7:4
does not have the Spirit of Christ does not **b** to him....8:9
They are Israelites, and to them **b** the adoption, .........9:4
To them **b** the patriarchs, and from their race, ............9:5
For not all who are descended from Israel **b** to Israel, .... 9:6
Greet those who **b** to the family of Aristobulus. .........16:10
in the Lord who **b** to the family of Narcissus. ............16:11

## BLESSED
rather than the Creator, who is **b** forever!................1:25
"**b** are those whose lawless deeds are forgiven, ...........4:7
**b** is the man against whom the Lord will not ....4:8
is the Christ, who is God over all, **b** forever................9:5
**b** is the one who has no reason to pass ................14:22

## BLOOD
"Their feet are swift to shed **b**; ................3:15

God put forward as a propitiation by his **b**,................3:25
therefore, we have now been justified by his **b**, ...........5:9

## BOAST
yourself a Jew and rely on the law and **b** in God.........2:17
You who **b** in the law dishonor God by breaking.........2:23
justified by works, he has something to **b** about, .........4:2

## BODY
weaken in faith when he considered his own **b**,........... 4:19
that the **b** of sin might be brought to nothing, .........6:6
Let not sin therefore reign in your mortal **b**,................6:12
also have died to the law through the **b** of Christ, ........7:4
Who will deliver me from this **b** of death?................7:24
although the **b** is dead because of sin, the Spirit ........8:10
you put to death the deeds of the **b**, you will live.......8:13
For as in one **b** we have many members,................12:4
so we, though many, are one **b** in Christ, ................12:5

## BRANCHES
and if the root is holy, so are the **b**................11:16
But if some of the **b** were broken off, ................11:17
do not be arrogant toward the **b**................11:18
"**B** were broken off so that I might be grafted............11:19
if God did not spare the natural **b**, neither will............11:21
the natural **b**, be grafted back into their own olive tree...11:24

## BROTHER
Why do you pass judgment on your **b**?................14:10
Or you, why do you despise your **b**?................14:10
stumbling block or hindrance in the way of a **b**............14:13
For if your **b** is grieved by what you eat,................14:15
or do anything that causes your **b** to stumble............14:21
city treasurer, and our **b** Quartus, greet you. ................16:23

## CALLS
and **c** into existence the things that do not exist.........4:17
not because of works but because of him who **c** .........9:11
"everyone who **c** on the name of the Lord will............10:13

## CAME
just as sin **c** into the world through one man,................5:12
Now the law **c** in to increase the trespass,................5:20
but when the commandment **c**, sin came alive ............7:9
commandment came, sin **c** alive and I died. ................7:9

## CIRCUMCISION
**c** indeed is of value if you obey the law, ................2:25
the law, your **c** becomes uncircumcision................2:25
not his uncircumcision be regarded as **c**?................2:26
you who have the written code and **c** but ................2:27
nor is **c** outward and physical................2:28
**c** is a matter of the heart, by the Spirit,................2:29
Or what is the value of **c**?................3:1
He received the sign of **c** as a seal of................4:11

## CLEAN
Everything is indeed **c**, but it is wrong for................14:20

## COMMANDMENT
seizing an opportunity through the **c**,................7:8
but when the **c** came, sin came alive ................7:9
The very **c** that promised life proved ................7:10
seizing an opportunity through the **c**,................7:11

## WITNESS

## WORD

## WORKS

## WORLD

## ZEAL